CHICAGO TRIAL TESTIMONY

Allen Ginsberg

City Lights

Library of Congress Cataloging in Publication Data

Ginsberg, Allen, 1926-
Chicago trial testimony.

Verbatim transcript of Allen Ginsberg's testimony as witness for the defendants (David T. Dellinger, et al.) in the 1969 "Chicago Seven" trial.
1. Ginsberg, Allen, 1926- 2. Dellinger, David T., 1915- 3. Chicago Riot, August, 1968.
I. Dellinger, David T., 1915- defendant. II. Title.
KF224.D37G45 345'.73'0231 74-31252
ISBN 0-87286-080-9

CITY LIGHTS BOOKS are published at the City Lights Bookstore.
Editorial & publishing offices: 1562 Grant Avenue, San Francisco, California 94133

THE 'CHICAGO SEVEN' TRIAL

UNITED STATES OF AMERICA

VS.

DAVID T. DELLINGER, et al.

DEFENDANTS:	David T. Dellinger Rennard C. Davis Abbott H. Hoffman Thomas E. Hayden Jerry C. Rubin Lee Weiner John R. Froines (Bobby G. Seale)
JUDGE:	Julius J. Hoffman
PROSECUTION:	Thomas Foran Richard G. Schultz Roger Cubbage
DEFENSE:	William Kunstler Leonard Weinglass
WITNESS FOR THE DEFENSE:	Allen Ginsberg

CHICAGO TRIAL TESTIMONY

This is the complete verbatim transcript of Allen Ginsberg's peace Conspiracy testimony as witness for Yippie-Activist-Pacifist defendants in 1969 *Chicago Seven* trial, presided over by the obstructive Judge Julius J. Hoffman.

This historical legal proceeding demonstrated a bodhisattvic attempt by the sub-culture spokesmen to communicate new consciousness to the entrenched establishment. Ginsberg's astute attempt to bridge the gap, typical of his special genius, climaxed with a loud OM silencing Judge and courtroom at moment of intemperate quarrel.

The poet's spontaneous exposition of psychedelic-sacred-sex revolutionary ecological background of Peace protest generation of 60's was one of high moment turning-points in profane trial which concluded with mostly innocent decision by Jury and helped collapse a series of Government conspiracy persecutions of Anti-war activist groups.

ALLEN GINSBERG

called as a witness on behalf of the defendants, having been first duly sworn, was examined and testified as follows:

DIRECT EXAMINATION

BY MR. WEINGLASS:

Q Will you please state your full name?

A Allen Ginsberg.

Q What is your occupation?

A Poet.

Q Have you authored any books in the field of poetry?

A Yes.

Q Will you indicate to the jury the titles of the books you have authored?

A In 1956, "Howl and Other Poems," in 1960, "Kaddish and Other Poems," in 1963, "Empty Mirror," in 1963, "Reality Sandwiches," and in 1968, "Planet News."

Q Now, in addition to your writing, Mr. Ginsberg, are you presently engaged in any other activity?

A I teach, lecture, and recite poetry at universities.

Q Can you indicate to the jury without going extensively into your travels what your last trip in connection with teaching and lecturing consisted of?

A I was at Princeton University for three days at the invitation of Reverend John Snow, the Episcopal Chaplain and Samuel, the Rabbi.

THE COURT: You will have to keep your voice up so that the reporter can record your testimony.

THE WITNESS: I was at Princeton University lecturing and teaching at the invitation of the Episcopal Chaplain, John Snow, and Rabbi Samuel.

BY MR. WEINGLASS:

Q And when were you at Princeton lecturing?

A Last week, the middle of last week.

Q Now, did you ever study abroad?

A Yes.

Q Where have you studied?

A In India and Japan.

Q Could you indicate for the Court and jury what the area of your studies consisted of?

A Mantra Yoga, meditation exercises, chanting, and sitting quietly, stilling the mind and breathing exercises to calm the body and to calm the mind, but mainly a branch called Mantra Yoga, which is a yoga which involves prayer and chanting.

Q How long did you study?

A I was in India for a year and a third, and then in Japan studying with Gary Snyder, a zen poet, at DaiTokuji Monastery, D-a-i-T-o-k-u-j-i. I sat there for the zazen sitting exercises for centering the body and quieting the mind.

Q Are you still studying under any of your former teachers?

A Yes, Swami Bhaktivedanta, faith, philosophy, Bhaktivedanta, B-h-a-k-t-i-v-e-d-a-n-t-a. I have seen him and chanted with him the last few years in different cities, and he has asked me to continue chanting especially on public occasions.

Q Have you received any special permission with respect to the chanting from the persons under whom you have studied?

A Yes, from Zen Master Roshi Suzuki, San Francisco Zen Buddhist Temple, who gave approval to my chanting of the Highest Perfect Wisdom Sutra, Prajna Paramita, P-r-a-j-n-a P-a-r-a-m-i-t-a, Prajna Paramita Sutra.

And also from Swami Satchitananda of New York, also from the school of Dr. Rammurti Mishra, D-r R-a-m-m-u-r-t-i M-i-s-h-r-a, a yogi who was the adviser of the New York Yoga Society, by whose disciples I have been initiated as a Shivit, S-h-i-v-i-t. That is a branch of Hinduism.

All of these involve chanting and praying, praying out loud and in community.

Q In the course of a Mantra chant, is there any particular position that the person doing that assumes?

A Any position which will let the stomach relax and be easy, fall out, so that inspiration can be deep into the body, to relax the body completely and calm the mind, based as cross-legged.

Q And is it, the chanting, to be done privately or is it in public?

MR. FORAN: Oh, your Honor, I object. I think we have gone far enough now to have established --

THE COURT: I think I have a vague idea of the witness' profession. It is vague.

MR. FORAN: I might indicate also that he is an excellent speller.

THE COURT: I sustain the objection, but I notice that he has said first he was a poet, and I will give him credit for all of the other things, too, whatever they are.

THE WITNESS: Sir --

THE COURT: Yes, sir.

THE WITNESS: In India, the profession of poetry and the profession of chanting are linked together as one practice.

THE COURT: That's right. I give you credit for that.

BY MR. WEINGLASS:

Q Mr. Ginsberg, do you know the defendant Jerry Rubin?

A Yes, I do.

Q Could you identify him seated here in this courtroom?

A Yes, the gentleman with the Indian headband.

Q How long have you known Jerry Rubin?

A Four and a half years.

Q Do you recall where it was that you first met him?

A In Berkeley and San Francisco in 1965 during the time of the anti-Vietnam war marches in Berkeley.

Q Were you associated with Mr. Rubin in that anti-war march?

A Yes, we worked together.

Q Did you have any further occasion in the year of 1967 to be associated with Mr. Rubin?

A Yes. I saw him again at the Human Be-in in San Francisco. We shared the stage with many other people.

Q Would you describe for the court and jury what the Be-in in San Francisco was?

A A large assembly of younger people who came together to --

MR. FORAN: Objection, your Honor.

THE COURT: Just a minute. I am not sure how you spell the Be-in

MR. WEINGLASS: B-E--I-N, I believe. Be-in.

THE WITNESS: Human Be-in.

THE COURT: I really can't pass on the validity of the objection because I don't understand the question.

MR. WEINGLASS: I asked him to explain what a Be-in was. I thought the question was directed to that possible confusion. He was interrupted in the course of the examination.

MR. FORAN: I would love to know also but I don't think it has anything to do with this lawsuit.

MR. WEINGLASS: Well, let's wait and find out.

MR. FORAN: This is San Francisco in 1967.

THE COURT: I will let him, over the objection of the government, tell what a Be-in is.

BY THE WITNESS:

A A gathering together of younger people aware of the planetary fate that we are all sitting in the middle of, imbued with a new consciousness and desiring of a new kind of society involving prayer, music and spiritual life together rather than competition, acquisition and war.

BY MR. WEINGLASS:

Q Did you have occasion -- and was that the activity that was engaged in in San Francisco at this Be-in?

A There was what was called a gathering of the tribes of all of the different affinity groups, political groups, spiritual groups, Yoga groups, music groups and poetry groups that all felt the same crisis of identity and crisis of the planet and political crisis in America, who all came together in the largest assemblage of such younger people that had taken place since the war in the presence of the Zen Master Suzuki that I mentioned before, in the presence of a number of Tibetan Buddhists and Japanese Zen Buddhists and in the presence of the rock bands and the presence of Timothy Leary and Mr. Rubin.

THE COURT: Now having had it explained to me, I will hear from you.

MR. FORAN: I object, your Honor.

THE COURT: I sustain the objection.

MR. FORAN: Your Honor, I will refrain from moving to have the jury directed to disregard it.

MR. WEINGLASS: If your Honor please --

MR. KUNSTLER: It isn't so funny that it has to be laughed at by the U.S. Attorney.

MR. FORAN: Your Honor --

MR. KUNSTLER: I think the objection can be stated --

THE WITNESS: Sir --

THE COURT: You will get another question.

MR. KUNSTLER: I will let Mr. Weinglass --

MR. WEINGLASS: In answering that objection, I think within the last hour the court has heard the prosecutor examine extensively a prior witness on another demonstration which occurred in October of 1967. I think we are talking about public meetings at which these defendants were present during the year 1967.

THE COURT: I will let my ruling stand. Ask another question.

BY MR. WEINGLASS:

Q Now during the -- later on in the year of 1967 did you have occasion to meet again with the defendant Jerry Rubin?

A Yes.

Q And what was that meeting concerning?

A We met in a cafe in Berkeley and discussed his mayoral race for the City of Berkeley. He had run for mayor.

Q Did you have any participation in that campaign?

A I encouraged it, blessed it.

Q Now do you know the defendant Abbie Hoffman?

A Yes.

Q Do you see him seated here at that table?

A Yes.

Q Would you identify him for the jury?

A At the corner of the table on your right with the wine-colored jacket.

Q For how long have you known Abbie Hoffman?

A Since late in 1967, I believe.

Q Now calling your attention to the month of February, 1968, did you have occasion in that month to meet with Abbie Hoffman?

A Yeah.

Q Do you recall the precise day of that meeting?

A No. Sometime mid-February, I think.

Q Do you recall where that meeting took place?

A In my apartment in New York.

Q Now were there any other persons present?

A No.

Q Did you have a conversation with Abbie Hoffman?

A Yes.

Q Could you relate to the jury what was discussed between you and Mr. Hoffman at that meeting?

A We talked about the possibility of extending the feeling of humanity and compassion of the Human Be-in in San Francisco to the City of Chicago during the time of the political convention, the possibility of inviting thc same kind of younger people and the same kind of teachers who had been at the San Francisco Human Be-in to Chicago at the time of the convention in order to show some different new planetary life style than was going to be shown to the younger people by the politicians who were assembling.

Q Now when you say, "We discussed," did Mr. Hoffman indicate to you what his intention was with respect to that discussion?

MR. FORAN: Objection, leading and suggestive.

THE COURT: I sustain the objection.

BY MR. WEINGLASS:

Q Do you recall what Mr. Hoffman said in the course of that conversation?

A Yippie -- among other things. He said that politics had become theatre and magic; that it was the manipulation of imagery through mass media that was confusing and hypnotizing the people in the United States and making them accept a war which they did not really believe in; that people were involved in a life style which was intolerable to the younger folk, which involved brutality and police violence as well as a larger violence in Viet Nam, and that ourselves might be able to get together in Chicago and invite teachers to present different ideas of what is wrong with the planet, what we can do to solve the pollution crisis, what we can do to solve the Viet Nam war, to present different ideas for making the society more sacred and less commercial, less materialistic, what we could do to uplevel or improve the whole tone of the trap that we all felt ourselves in as the population grew and as politics became more and more violent and chaotic.

Q Did he mention to you specifically any teachers that he had in mind for coming to Chicago?

MR. FORAN: Objection.

THE COURT: I sustain the objection.

BY MR. WEINGLASS:

Q Did you hear him mention the names of Mr. Burroughs, Mr. Olson and other teachers?

A Burroughs, Olson and Mr. Fuller.

THE COURT: Mr. Witness --

MR. FORAN: Objection to the leading and suggestive question.

THE COURT: I sustain the objection and I strike the answer and direct the jury to disregard it.

BY MR. WEINGLASS:

Q Mr. Ginsberg, does your prior answer exhaust your recollection as to what Mr. Hoffman said at that meeting?

A Yes.

Q Do you recall him mentioning anything about any rock and roll bands?

A Yes.

Q What did he say about rock and roll bands?

A Well, he said that he was in contact with John Sinclair who was the leader of the MC 5 rock and roll band and John Sinclair and Ed Sanders of the Fugs would collaborate together and invite a lot of rock and roll people, popular music such as Arlo Guthrie -- Phil Ochs was also mentioned by Mr. Hoffman. Mr. Hoffman asked me if I could contact the Beatles or Bob Dylan and tell them what was afoot and ask them if they could join us so that we could actually put on a really beautiful thing that would turn everybody on in the sense of like uplift everybody's spirit and show actually what we were actually feeling as far as delight instead of the horror that was surrounding us.

Q Now did he ascribe any particular name to that project?

A Festival of Life.

Q Did he ask you to take any active role in the Festival of Life?

MR. FORAN: Objection, your Honor. Can't Mr. Weinglass --

THE COURT: I sustain the objection.

MR. FORAN: I mean, those are all leading and suggestive questions, your Honor, and I object to them. They are improper.

THE COURT: I have already sustained the objection.

BY MR. WEINGLASS:

Q After he spoke to you, what, if anything was your response to his suggestion?

A I was worried as to whether or not the whole scene would get violent. I was worried whether we would be allowed to put on such a situation. I was worried whether, you know, the Government would let us do something that was funnier or prettier or more charming than what was going to be going on in the convention hall.

MR. FORAN: I object and ask that it be stricken. It was not responsive.

THE COURT: Yes. I sustain the objection.

THE WITNESS: Sir, this is -- that was our conversation.

THE COURT: I direct the jury to disregard the last answer of the witness.

MR. WEINGLASS: Your Honor, I would like to --

THE WITNESS: How can I phrase that then because that was our --

MR. WEINGLASS: Your Honor, I would like to be informed by the Court how that answer was not responsive to that question. It seemed to me to be directly responsive.

MR. FORAN: Your Honor, he asked him what he said and he answered by saying what he was wondering.

THE COURT: Worry.

THE WITNESS: Oh, I am sorry, then. I said to Jerry that I was worried about violence --

THE COURT: I have ruled on the objection. Ask another question if you like.

BY MR. WEINGLASS:

Q Now during that same month, February of 1968, did you have occasion to meet with Jerry Rubin?

A I spoke to Jerry Rubin on the phone, I believe.

Q Did you call him or did he call you?

A I called him.

Q Do you recall where you called him at?

A His house, his apartment on the Lower East Side in New York.

Q Did you have his home phone number?

A Yes.

Q Was it that number that you dialed?

A Yes.

Q And who answered?

A Jerry did. I asked if could speak with Jerry Rubin and he said "That's me," and I recognized his voice.

Q Had you talked to Jerry Rubin prior to this occasion by telephone?

Q Yes, often.

Q How many times approximately had you talked to him before by telephone since knowing him?

A Oh, ten, twelve.

Q Could you recognize his voice?

A Yes.

Q Did you recognize his voice in the course of this telephone conversation?

A Yes.

Q Now do you recall what was discussed during that telephone conversation?

A Yes.

Q Will you relate to the Court and jury what Jerry Rubin said to you.

A Jerry told me that he and others were going to Chicago to apply for permission from the city government for a permit to hold a Festival of Life and that he was talking with John Sinclair about getting rock and roll bands together and other musicians and that he would report back to me and try to find a good place near where we could either meet delegates and influence delegates or where we could have like some kind of central location in the city where people could sleep overnight so we could actually invite younger people to come or come ourselves with knapsacks and sleeping bags, somewhat as turned out at the Woodstock Festival this year.

MR. FORAN: I object to this, your Honor. He would have had a hard time saying that.

THE COURT: The reference to the Woodstock Festival may go out and the jury is directed to disregard it.

THE WITNESS: Sir, the imagination that we had of it --

THE COURT: Will you excuse me, sir? I am not permitted to engage in a colloquy with the witness.

THE WITNESS: I am just trying to clarify the data that I know.

THE COURT: A lawyer is asking you questions. You just answer them as best you can.

BY MR. WEINGLASS:

Q Did Mr. Rubin in the course of that conversation indicate what activities were planned for Chicago during the Democratic Convention?

A Yes. He said that he thought it would be interesting if we could set up tents and areas within the park where kids could come and sleep, and set up little schools like ecology schools, music schools, political schools, schools about the Viet Nam war, to go back into history, schools with yogis.
He suggested that I contact whatever professional breathing - exercise Yogi Swami teachers I could find and invite them to Chicago and asked if I could contact Burroughs and ask Burroughs to come also to teach non-verbal, non-conceptual feeling states.

Q Now you indicated a school of ecology. Could you explain to the Court and jury what that is?

A Ecology is the interrelation of all the living forms on the surface of the planet involving the food chain, - that is to say, whales eat plankton; littler organisms in the ocean eat tiny microscopic organisms called plankton; larger fishes eat smaller fish; octopus or squid eat shellfish which eat plankton; human beings eat the shellfish or squid or smaller fish which eat the smaller tiny micro-organisms.

MR. FORAN: That is enough, your Honor.

THE COURT: You say that is enough?

MR. FORAN: I think that the question is now responsive. I think that --

THE COURT: Yes. We all have a clear idea now of what ecology is.

THE WITNESS: Well, the destruction of ecology is what would have been taught. That is, how it is being destroyed by human intervention and messing it up with pollution.

BY MR. WEINGLASS:

Q Now you also indicated that Mr. Rubin mentioned non-verbal education. Will you explain what that is to the Court and jury.

A Most of our consciousness, since we are continually looking at images on television and listening to words, reading newspapers, talking in courts as this, most of our consciousness is filled with language, with a kind of matter babble behind the ear, a continuous yackety-yack that actually prevents us from breathing deeply in our bodies and sensing more subtly and sweetly the feelings that we actually do have as persons to each other rather than as to talking machines.

Q Now, Mr. Ginsberg, on March 17, 1968, where were you?

A I took part in a press conference at the Hotel Americana.

Q In what city is that?

A New York City.

Q Who else was present at this press conference?

A Abbie Hoffman and Jerry Rubin were there as well as Phil Ochs, the folk singer, Arlo Guthrie, some members of the USA Band, Bob Fass, who was a sort of Hip psychedelic radio announcer on the FM stations and a leader of the intellectual culture in New York was there; some members of the Diggers groups.

Q At this press conference were there cameras there?

A Yes, there was national television.

Q And will you explain to the Court and jury what the purpose of the press conference was?

MR. FORAN: I object to that, your Honor.

THE COURT: I have to sustain the objection.

BY MR. WEINGLASS:

Q Now at that press conference did you hear Jerry Rubin speak?

A Yes.

Q Could you indicate to the Court and jury what Jerry Rubin said?

A He announced the Yippie Festival of Life to the nation and said that he was going to Chicago during the convention time and hoped that a lot of younger people in America would come to the convention, come to Chicago during the convention and hold a Festival of Life in the parks, and he announced that they were negotiating with the City Hall to get a permit to have a life festival in the parks.

Q Did you hear Abbie Hoffman speak at that press conference?

A Yes.

Q Do you recall what Abbie Hoffman said?

A He talked a lot about -- he said that they were negotiating with -- were going to go to Chicago in a group to negotiate with representatives of Mayor Daley to get a permit for a large-scale gathering of the tribes and he mentioned the Human Be-in in San Francisco.

Q Did you yourself participate in that press conference?

A Yes. I stepped to the microphone also.

Q At whose request did you participate?

A Abbie Hoffman asked me to make a statement.

Q And did you make a statement?

A Yes.

Q Will you explain to the Court and jury what your statement was?

A My statement --

MR. FORAN: I object to him explaining what it was. He can give what he said.

MR. WEINGLASS: Could I have the basis of the objection?

MR. FORAN: You asked, "Would you explain what your statement was."

MR. WEINGLASS: Oh, I am sorry.

BY MR. WEINGLASS:

Q Would you explain what your statement was.

A My statement was that the planet Earth at the present moment was endangered by violence, over-population, pollution, ecological destruction brought about by our own greed; that the younger children in America and other countries of the world might not survive the next 30 years, that it was a planetary crisis that had not been recognized by any government of the world and had not been recognized by our own government, nor the politicians who were preparing for the elections; that the younger people of America were aware of that and that precisely was what was called pyschedelic consciousness; that we were going to gather together as we had before in the San Francisco Human Be-in to manifest our presence over and above the presence of the more selfish elder politicians who were not thinking in terms of what their children would need in future generations or even in the generation immediately coming or even for themselves in their own lifetime and were continuing to threaten the planet with violence, with war, with mass murder, with germ warfare, and since the younger people knew that in the United States, we were going to invite them there and that the central motive would be a presentation of a desire for the preservation of the planet. The desire for preservation of the planet and the planet's form, that we do continue to be, to exist on this planet instead of destroy the planet, was manifested to my mind by the great Mantra, from India, to the preserver God Vishnu---whose Mantra is Hare Krishna; and then I chanted the Hare Krishna Mantra for ten minutes to the television cameras and it goes:

"Hare Krishna, Hare Krishna, Krishna Krishna, Hare Hare,
Hare Rama, Hare Rama, Rama Rama, Hare Hare."

Q Now in chanting that did you have an accompaniment of any particular instrument?

MR. FORAN: Objection as immaterial. He wants to know if there was accompaniment of an instrument.

THE COURT: By an instrument do you mean --

MR. KUNSTLER: Your Honor, I object to the laughter of the Court on this. I think this is a serious presentation of a religious concept.

THE COURT: I don't understand it. I don't understand it because it was -- the language of the United States District Court is English.

MR. KUNSTLER: I know, but you don't laugh at all languages.

THE WITNESS: I would be glad to explain it, sir.

THE COURT: I didn't laugh. I didn't laugh.

THE WITNESS: I would be happy to explain it.

THE COURT: I didn't laugh at all. I wish I could tell you how I feel. Laugh, I didn't even smile.

MR. KUNSTLER: Well, I thought --

THE COURT: All I could tell you is that I didn't understand it because whatever language the witness used --

THE WITNESS: Sanskrit, sir.

THE COURT: What is it?

THE WITNESS: Sanskrit, sir.

THE COURT: Sanskrit?

THE WITNESS: Yes.

THE COURT: Well, that is one I don't know. That is the reason I didn't understand it.

THE WITNESS: There is a popular song put out by the Beatles with those words.

THE COURT: I am not interested in --

MR. FORAN: Your Honor, of course the laughter came from everybody that Mr. Kunstler is usually defending for laughing.

MR. KUNSTLER: Your Honor, I would say -- You mean from the press?

THE WITNESS: Might we go on to an explanation.

THE COURT: Will you keep quiet, Mr. Witness, while I am talking to the lawyers?

THE WITNESS: I will be glad to give an explanation.

THE COURT: I never laugh at a witness, sir. I protect witnesses who come to this court. They are entitled to the protection of the Court. But I do tell you that as I am sure you know, the language of American courts is English. The English language, unless we have an interpreter. You may use an interpreter for the remainder of this witness' testimony.

MR. KUNSTLER: No. I have heard, your Honor, priests explain the mass in Latin in American courts and I think Mr. Ginsberg is doing exactly the same thing in Sanskrit for another type of religious experience.

THE COURT: No, no. You are mistaken.

MR. KUNSTLER: Your Honor, I can't --

THE COURT: I don't understand Sanskrit. I venture to say the members of the jury don't. Perhaps we have some people on the jury who do understand Sanskrit, I don't know, but I wouldn't even have known it was Sanskrit until he told me.

MR. KUNSTLER: Your Honor, I don't think it is being offered for people to understand the literal meaning of the words. It is being offered as an example of what he did before national television.

THE COURT: I can't see that that is material to the issues here, that is all.

MR. WEINGLASS: Let me ask this:

Mr. Ginsberg, I show you an object marked 150 for identification, and I ask you to examine that object.

A Yes. (Plays C chord)

MR. FORAN: All right.

Your Honor, that is enough. I object to it, your Honor. I think that it is outrageous for counsel to --

THE COURT: You asked him to examine it and instead of that he played a tune on it.

MR. FORAN: I mean, counsel is so clearly --

THE COURT: I sustain the objection.

MR. FORAN: -- talking about things that have no conceivable materiality to this case, and it is improper, your Honor.

THE WITNESS: It adds spirituality to the case, sir.

THE COURT: Will you remain quiet, sir.

THE WITNESS: I am sorry.

THE COURT: My obligation is to protect you, but my obligation is to see that you act in accordance with the law.

THE WITNESS: I agree, sir.

BY MR. WEINGLASS:

Q Having examined that, could you identify it for the Court and the jury?

MR. FORAN: I object to it. It is immaterial.

MR WEINGLASS: I am not offering it. It is an exhibit marked for identification. We are entitled to have it identified.

THE COURT: You are entitled to have it identified. What is it?

THE WITNESS: It is an instrument known as the Harmonium, which I used at the press conference at the Americana Hotel.

THE COURT: All you were asked was what is it, sir?

THE WITNESS: It is a musical instrument which is used to accompany Mantra chanting, to accompany the chanting of the Hare Krishna Mantra, and other Mantra. It is commonly used in India --

THE COURT: You have answered that, sir.

MR. FORAN: I object to that.

THE COURT: I sustain the objection.

BY MR. WEINGLASS:

Q Now in the Mantra chanted at the press conference, were you accompanied with that instrument?

A I was accompanying myself on that instrument. I was chanting, rather than pronouncing it as I did before. I pronounced it before. At the press conference, I chanted.

Q Will you explain to the Court and to the jury what chant you were chanting at the press conference?

A I was chanting a Mantra called the Maha Mantra, the Great Mantra of Preservation of that aspect of the Indian religion called Vishnu, the Preserver, whom every time human evil, human evil rises so high that the planet itself is threatened, and all of its inhabitants and their children are threatened, Vishnu will return and preserve.

MR. FORAN: I object to that.

THE COURT: Oh, yes, I sustain the objection, and I strike the answer of the witness. I direct the jury to disregard it.
When you offer anything in a foreign language, sir, and you think it is material, you must have an interpreter here so that the witness can be --

THE WITNESS: Sir, it is a legal record here.

THE COURT: Did you hear what I said earlier to you?

THE WITNESS: Yes.

MR. WEINGLASS: If the Court please, I do have an interpreter. The interpreter happens to be the witness.

THE COURT: Oh, no, that would hardly be fair. An interpreter must be responsible to the Court, and he must take a special oath. I don't know whether you know that or not, but we have a special oath here for interpreters.

MR. WEINGLASS: It is my understanding that an interpreter is only used when the witness is not proficient in the English language and requires the aid of an interpreter.

THE COURT: He used another language here.

MR. WEINGLASS: And he has the capacity to explain it to the jury. Therefore, an interpreter is not necessary.

THE COURT: It is impossible to cross-examine a man when he is using Sanskrit which is a language --

THE WITNESS: I am speaking English, sir.

THE COURT: -- which is not used.

Now, I have tried to be as kind as I could to you.

THE WITNESS: I am trying to be kind to you.

THE COURT: I don't want you to interrupt me when I am speaking.

Ladies and gentlemen of the jury, we are going to recess now until ten o'clock tomorrow morning. My usual orders, I direct you not to talk with anybody about this case, not to let anybody speak with you about it. Do not discuss the case among yourselves. If anybody attempts to communicate with you about this case in any manner whatsoever, get in touch with the United States Marshal, who will in turn lay the matter before me. I order you not to read the newspapers or any other journals, not to listen to radio or television, or to look at television.

Mr. Witness, we are about to recess until ten o'clock tomorrow morning. I order you to return here tomorrow morning at ten o'clock for further examination. I also order you not to talk with anybody about this case or let anybody speak with you about it until you resume the stand at ten o'clock tomorrow morning.

THE WITNESS: Pardon me, does that include the lawyers.

THE MARSHAL: Everyone please rise.

MR. FORAN: Your Honor, the witness had a question.

THE COURT: What is your question?

THE WITNESS: Does that include the lawyers for the defense?

THE COURT: That most certainly does. You are not to talk to anybody. You are not to talk to anybody about this case or let anybody speak with you about it.

(Whereupon an adjournment was taken to 10:00 a.m., of the following day, Friday, December 12, 1969.)

IN THE UNITED STATES DISTRICT COURT
NORTHERN DISTRICT OF ILLINOIS
EASTERN DIVISION

UNITED STATES OF AMERICA	)	
vs.	)	69 CR 180
	)	
DAVID T. DELLINGER, et al.,	)	
Defendants.	)	
	)	

Before Judge Hoffman and a Jury,
Friday, December 12, 1969,
10:00 o'clock a.m.

Trial resumed pursuant to adjournment.

Present:

Mr. Foran
Mr. Schultz
Mr. Cubbage

Mr. Kunstler
Mr. Weinglass

THE CLERK: No. 69 CR 180. United States of America vs. David T. Dellinger, et al. Cause on trial.

(The following proceedings were had in open court, out of the presence and hearing of the jury:)

THE CLERK: Motion of Marshall Patner for leave to appear as additional counsel and motion to extend time for filing record on appeal to January 15.

MR. PATNER: This is in the Bobby Seale matter. My name is Marshall Patner. I have attached a copy of a letter to Mr. McTernan authorizing me to appear as additional counsel for the purpose of getting the record on appeal up if that motion is granted. I have a motion to extend time for filing the record on appeal to and including January 15th.

THE COURT: Mr. Patner, in ordinary circumstances I would allow a motion like this routinely, but you have not served all counsel of record.
If you will look at the record, serve them, come in with proof of service, and I will be glad to --

MR. PATNER: Do you mean counsel for the defendants?

THE COURT: Yes.

MR. PATNER: All counsel for the defendants?

THE COURT: All counsel for the defendants, sir.

MR. PATNER: What will you do, enter and continue this, then, your Honor?

THE COURT: Yes. I will be glad to do it, sir. There is of record an appearance here for Mr. Seale by two others lawyers whom you have not served.

MR. PATNER: Shall I just notice it up for another day or do you want me to set it sometime.

THE COURT: You notice it up beacuse you may want to arrange with the lawyers for a convenient time. I will be here so it doesn't matter what morning you choose.
I suggest you withdraw the motion at this time so there will be no minute order necessary.

MR. PATNER: All right. I will do that.

THE CLERK: All of the defendants are not here.

THE COURT: Are the parties ready in this case?

MR. KUNSTLER: Your Honor, just one preliminary matter: Mr. Weiner last night had his glasses broken and finds it difficult to see without them and needs -- what is it, a half hour?

MR. WEINER: About 45 minutes.

MR. KUNSTLER: He needs about 45 minutes this morning to get his lenses repaired. I would just ask your Honor's indulgence. He will waive any right to be here. I don't think there will be any testimony concerning him.

THE COURT: Whose glasses were broken?

MR. KUNSTLER: Mr. Weiner. He just wants to --

THE COURT: Is there any objection on the part of the government?

MR. FORAN: No. We have no objection to that, your Honor, as long as Mr. Weiner --

THE COURT: Mr. Weiner, your lawyer, Mr. Kunstler, has requested the court to allow you to go some place. I interpret the motion to mean to get your glasses repaired or get new glasses. The government does not have objection. Do you waive your constitutional right to be present during that period which I am told will be about 45 minutes?

MR. WEINER: Allen could never hurt me. Yes.

THE COURT: I didn't hear that.

MR. WEINER: Allen could never hurt me and I would waive my right.

THE COURT: Who couldn't hurt you?

MR. WEINER: Allen who will be testifying. Yes, sir, I waive my right.

THE COURT: I don't understand that, but as long as you say you waive your constitutional right to be present --

MR. KUNSTLER: Thank you, your Honor.

MR. WEINER: Thank you.

THE MARSHAL: The defendants will please keep quiet, please.

THE COURT: Mr. Marshal, are the defendants here other than Mr. Weiner?

THE MARSHAL: Yes, your Honor.

THE COURT: Bring in the jury, then, please.

(The following proceedings were had in open court, in the presence and hearing of the jury:)

THE COURT: Ladies and gentlemen of the jury, good morning. Will the witness please resume the stand.

ALLEN GINSBERG,

a witness called by and on behalf of the defendants herein, having been previously duly sworn, resumed the stand, was examined and testified further as follows:

THE COURT: You may continue, sir, with the direct examination of this witness.

DIRECT EXAMINATION
(Resumed:)

BY MR. WEINGLASS:

Q Mr. Ginsberg, when we left off yesterday you were testifying about a statement and a chant which you sang at a press conference on March 17, 1968. Do you recall that?

A Yes, sir.

Q I show you a document marked D-151 for identification, and I ask you if you could identify that document.

A Yes.

Q Can you tell the Court and jury what that document is?

A It is the stationery of the Youth International Party, Yippies, Festival of Life office in Union Square in New York.

Q Have you seen that stationery before?

A Yes, a few times.

MR. WEINGLASS: If the Court please, the document has been handed to the Government and at this point I offer Defendants' D-151 for identification into evidence as Defendants' Exhibit D-151.

MR. FORAN: We have no objection.

THE COURT: With no objection, Defendants' Exhibit 151 for identification may be admitted into evidence as Defendants' Exhibit 151.

(Whereupon said exhibit, so offered and received in evidence, was marked Defendants' Exhibit 151 in evidence.)

BY MR. WEINGLASS:

Q Now, Mr. Ginsberg, directing your attention to the top of that document, is there a heading on the stationery indicating the source of the document at the top of the document?

A "Festival of Life" is what it says.

Q Is that what appears?

A Yes.

Q Going down the left-hand column of that document, is there a list of names?

A Yes, there is a list of names of people who are cooperating with the Festival of Life.

Q In looking down that list, does your name appear?

MR. FORAN: Your Honor, I object to that description.

THE COURT: You mean the words "Who are cooperating"?

MR. FORAN: Yes, your Honor.

THE COURT: Those words do not appear on the exhibit? I will look at the exhibit.

MR. WEINGLASS: Those words do not appear.

THE COURT: If they do not appear, Mr. Weinglass, I will strike the words "those who are cooperating" and any words that followed and direct the jury to disregard them.

BY MR. WEINGLASS:

Q Now looking down the list of persons who appear on the left-hand column, does your name appear?

A Yes.

Q Under what particular topical heading does your name appear?

A Religion.

Q Are you listed there alone under religion or are there other persons listed also?

A Paul Krassner and Timothy Leary are also listed.

Q Now at the bottom of that document is there any indication as to the source of the document?

A Youth International Party, 32 Union Square East, New York, New York, with a phone number.

Q Looking at the top of the document, the left-hand column, is there a category indicated?

A Yes. Music.

Q Music. And then is there another category listed under that?

A Theatre.

Q And another category listed under that?

A Art.

Q Another one under that?

A Newspaper.

Q Under that?

A Religion.

Q Under that?

A Film.

Q The next?

A Sex.

Q And the last one?

A Games.

Q And your name appears in which category?

A The religion category.

Q Could you read the people who appear in the first category?

A Under music, Jerry Brandt, Judy Collins, Al Cooper, Bob Fass, Michael Goldstein, Richard Goldstein, Bill Graham, Harold Leventhal, Joe MacDonald, Michael Ochs, Ellen Sander, Ed Sanders, Jack Solomon and Andy Wickham.

Q In the next category?

A Under Theatre, Eric Bentley, Ed Bullins, Jim Fouratt, Saul Gottlieb, Allan Kaprow, Jacques Levy, Robert Macbeth, John O'Neal, Richard Schechner, Peter Schumann, Enrique Vargas and Douglas Turner Ward.

Q And the next category?

A Art: Diane diPrima, Gary Grimshaw, George Herms, Tiger Morse, Carol Shebar, Gerd Stern, Jud Yalkut.

Q And the next?

A Newspaper: Ed Beardsley, Marshall Bloom, John Bryant, Allen Cohen, Marvin Garson, Martin Jeezer, Alan Katzman, Ray Mungo, Collin Pearson and Max Scheer.

Q You may skip the category of religion; you have already indicated that. Move to the next.

A Film: Joe Cohen, Marvin Fishman, Norm Fruchter, Peter Gessner.

Q And the next?

A Sex: Tuli Kupferberg, Alan Marlowe.

Q And the next category?

A Games: Abbie Hoffman, Keith Lampe, Abe Peckolick, Hugh Romney, Jerry Rubin and Gloria Yippie.

Q Will you describe that list of persons -- would you describe that list of persons as a respresentative list of people who represented the underground youth culture?

MR. FORAN: Objection.

THE COURT: I sustain the objection.

BY MR. WEINGLASS:

Q Directing your attention to the month of April, 1965, did you have occasion during that month to meet with the defendant Jerry Rubin?

A Yes.

Q Do you recall what particular day it was that you met with him?

A No. Mid-April, I guess.

Q Where was that meeting?

A At my house.

Q Was there anyone else present?

A No.

Q During the course of that meeting did you have a conversation with Mr. Rubin?

A Yes.

Q What did that conversation concern?

MR. FORAN: I object to that, your Honor.

THE COURT: The form is bad. I will sustain the objection.

BY MR. WEINGLASS:

Q What was the substance of that conversation, Mr. Ginsberg?

MR. FORAN: Objection to that, your Honor.

THE COURT: I sustain the objection.

BY MR. WEINGLASS:

Q Now in the course of that meeting, what, if anything, did Jerry Rubin say?

A He said that he wanted to be sure that there would be a large gathering in Chicago of younger people who could get together to continue the tradition of the be-in that we had participated in before; that in order to insure that it be a peaceful gathering so that a lot of people would come, encouraged by the air of peacefulness of it, that it be a festival of life, they were applying as a group to the Chicago Mayor's office to get a permit for a gathering but that apparently they were having trouble getting the permit, they hadn't been assured of a permit for the gathering yet and they would continue negotiating with the city, with City Hall for that permit.

Then I asked him what his personal intentions were for the Festival of Life, how he felt about it, what he wanted out of it, and he said he felt it was necessary that a lot of people come; that the only way a lot of people would come is if there were really good vibrations coming out of us and that he wanted it to be a peaceful gathering.

I asked him that specifically because I was scared --

MR. FORAN: Objection.

BY THE WITNESS:

A I told him I was scared --

MR. FORAN: Objection to why, your Honor.

THE COURT: "I asked him that specifically," those words may go out and the jury is directed to disregard them.

BY THE WITNESS:

A I told him that I was scared of getting into a scene where I would get beaten up or a mob scene because I was not used to that and I didn't want to. I was just simply frightened of too large a gathering which would involve conflict and fighting and getting my head busted in, and so I asked him how he felt about it, whether he was going to work for an actually peaceful gathering or not, because I didn't want to participate unless it was going to be organized peacefully, and he said he wanted it to be peaceful because he wanted a lot of people there.

BY MR. WEINGLASS:

Q Now in the early part of August, 1968, did you have occasion to talk with the defendant Abbie Hoffman?

A Yes.

Q Was this a personal meeting or was this by other means of communication?

A By telephone.

Q Do you recall where you were?

A In San Francisco.

Q Did you call Abbie Hoffman or did Abbie Hoffman call you?

A I think he called me.

Q When he called you, did he identify himself on the telephone?

A Yes.

Q Had you talked with Abbie Hoffman before this by telephone?

A Yes.

Q Could you recognize and identify his voice?

A Yes.

Q On the day of the telephone conversation we are referring to, could you recognize the voice at the other end of the phone as being that of Abbie Hoffman?

A Yes.

Q Now will you relate to the jury what Abbie Hoffman said to you in the course of that telephone conversation?

MR. FORAN: Could we pin the date down a little?

MR. WEINGLASS: I will try.

Q Do you remember whether that was the first half of August or the last half of August?

A Early August, around, I think, the 8th or 9th.

Q Do you recall what Abbie Hoffman said to you in that telephone conversation?

A I asked him if he had gotten a permit for the meeting yet or whether the Yippies had gotten a permit from City Hall and he said so far no. He said that he had talked with David Stahl in the Mayor's office, that there had been many conversations, but that Stahl had not absolutely refused but had refused so far and that they were still --

MR. FORAN: Your Honor, I object to this. This is just hearsay. This is not --

THE COURT: I sustain the objection. "He had talked with David Stahl," those words and the words that followed may go out and the jury is directed to disregard them.

BY MR. WEINGLASS:

Q Without referring to any conversation that Mr. Hoffman might have told you he had with a third person, could you go on and tell the jury what Mr. Hoffman said to you on the telephone?

A He said literally, "The city officials are not granting us a permit and are hanging us up and dangling it in front of us and trying to discourage us from having a public assembly in Chicago during the time of the convention," that he would continue applying to City Hall for permission and that possibly they might even call off the festival if they absolutely could not get permission, but would continue to the last day applying and try to get cooperation from the city.

Q Now does that exhaust your recollection as to what Abbie Hoffman told you on the telephone that day?

A No. He told me that if I were coming east, could I stop in Chicago and check out the scene with people here and go visit City Hall and talk with Mr. Stahl.

Q And what did you say in reply to that?

A I said I wasn't sure but I would try. If I could get a plane ticket from San Francisco to New York that would stop over in Chicago, I would stop over for a day and visit everybody I could because I was a little scared -- I told him I was scared so I wanted to look out, gaze out over the scene, because I hadn't been in Chicago in a long time. I wanted to see what it was like, what the streets were like, what the people were like, and also if I could make a date with the Mayor's office and talk with him.

Q Following that conversation did you come to the City of Chicago?

A Yes, I did.

Q Did you come here from San Francisco?

A Yes.

Q Do you recall the date that you arrived in Chicago?

A April 12, 1968.

Q Do you mean August or April?

A August. I am sorry.

Q Now directing your attention to the following day which is August 13th at approximately 5:30 in the afternoon, where were you in the City of Chicago?

A I went up to City Hall to the Mayor's office.

Q Did you meet with anyone in the Mayor's office in City Hall?

A I met with Mr. Stahl who said he was the Mayor's assistant.

Q Was there anyone else present?

A Yes. Mr. Stahl asked if I would mind talking in front of Earl Bush who he said was the Mayor's public relations assistant.

Q Was this a meeting of just the three of you or were there other persons as well?

A It was only the three of us.

Q Approximately how long did this meeting last?

A It went on for a couple of hours, two hours, an hour and a half.

Q In the course of this meeting could you relate to the jury what you said to Mr. Stahl?

MR. FORAN: Objection. Hearsay.

THE COURT: I sustain the objection.

MR. WEINGLASS: I asked what he said to Mr. Stahl. It is not hearsay. I didn't ask him what Mr. Stahl said to him.

THE COURT: You may comment on that.

MR. FORAN: Your Honor, it doesn't make any difference. The whole conversation has not got any direct link-up to this case.

THE COURT: I sustain the objection. I will let my ruling stand.

MR. WEINGLASS: Your Honor, do I understand that this witness cannot testify as to what he said? He could be cross-examined on it.

THE COURT: You understand that I have sustained the objection.

MR. WEINGLASS: I want to make it clear I am not asking for what Mr. Stahl said.

THE COURT: I am listening very carefully, sir.

MR. WEINGLASS: Well, when the witness Baugher was on the stand and Stahl, they were permitted to testify what they said in conversations.

THE COURT: I will let my ruling stand. You may continue with your direct examination.

BY MR. WEINGLASS:

Q Now disregarding any conversation or any talk you might have had with

Mr. Stahl and Mr. Bush, could you relate to the jury what, if anything, occurred in the course of that meeting?

A We talked for two hours. I told Mr. Stahl that I was afraid of getting into a violent scene --

MR. FORAN: I object, your Honor. There are no defendants present at this conversation.

THE COURT: I sustain the objection.

MR. WEINGLASS: There doesn't have to be. The witness is just relating what he said and he can be cross-examined on what he said. There is no infirmity in his testimony.

THE COURT: I will let my ruling stand.

BY MR. WEINGLASS:

Q Not going into any conversation, Mr. Ginsberg, did anything occur or happen during the course of this meeting?

A I chanted the Hare Krishna Mantra to Mr. Stahl and Mr. Bush as an example of what was intended by the Festival of Life and I asked them to please give a permit to avoid violence.

MR. FORAN: I object to that and I ask that it be stricken.

THE COURT: The last words of the witness may go out and the jury is directed to disregard them.

BY MR. WEINGLASS:

Q Can you indicate to the court and jury what the Mantra Hare Krishna is?

MR. FORAN: I object to that, your Honor. He can say what he did.

THE COURT: I sustain the objection.

BY MR. WEINGLASS:

Q What, Mr. Ginsberg, is the purpose of the chanting of the Mantra Hare Krishna?

MR. FORAN: I object to that.

THE COURT: I sustain the objection.

BY MR. WEINGLASS:

Q Could you chant for the court and the jury the Mantra Hare Krishna as you did that day?

MR. FORAN: Objection.

THE COURT: I sustain the objection.

BY MR. WEINGLASS:

Q Could you speak without chanting for the court and jury the Mantra Hare Krishna?

A Hare Krishna, Hare Krishna --

MR. FORAN: Your Honor --

THE COURT: Just a minute.

MR. FORAN: May I have the question?

THE COURT: Read the question

(Question read.)

MR. FORAN: I object.

THE COURT: I sustain the objection.

BY MR. WEINGLASS:

Q After this meeting in City Hall, Mr. Ginsberg, did you have occasion to meet on that same day any of the defendants in this case?

A Yes.

Q Who did you meet?

A Abbie Hoffman.

Q With relationship to this meeting with Mr. Stahl, approximately how long after your City Hall meeting did you meet with Abbie Hoffman?

A Directly afterward I went to the place where Abbie Hoffman was staying for supper.

Q Did Abbie Hoffman have a conversation with you that meeting?

A Yes.

Q Could you relate to the court and jury what Abbie Hoffman said to you at that meeting?

A He said that all along the City Hall representatives of the Mayor had refused to give permission outright, had occasionally offered different possibilities for meeting places in the city but nothing definite had resulted; that he felt he was being given a run-around; they were dangling Democratic procedure before the Yippie group for the Festival of Life but were not allowing a peaceful assembly under constitutional propriety; that he did not know what to do except that many people were intending to come in any case to Chicago since from a half a year resolution this had been taken by many people to come to Chicago.

He asked me if I was going to come and I said yes, I felt obligated to come since from the very beginning I had put my name forward as one of the people cooperating with the Yippies and therefore I had a responsibility to go there even if it was going to be dangerous because other young people were coming in my name or coming because I had said I was coming, so that I felt obligated by duty to go there and make sure it was as peaceful as possible.

He also asked me --

MR. FORAN: I object to this, your Honor, as all non-responsive. He was asked to relate what Hoffman said, and he is giving now a ten-minute dissertation or a long statement.

THE COURT: Yes, I must make sure that the witness is testifying that that is what Mr. Hoffman said. He said all of that?

THE WITNESS: He said all of that up to where -- am I to respond to him?

THE COURT: The responses of the witness may go out and the jury is directed to disregard them.

BY MR. WEINGLASS:

Q Mr. Ginsberg, does that exhaust your recollection of what Mr. Hoffman said to you?

A He asked me what my conversation was with Mr. Stahl and Mr. Bush.

Q Now you are not permitted to relate that. Aside from that, does that exhaust your recollection of what Abbie Hoffman said to you at that meeting?

A He said that the park at Lincoln Park had been divided up into different areas for theatre, for theatre school, for training in free theatre, for training in first aid, in case the younger people were attacked, for a music area, a motor bike persons' area, a free store, a booth to indicate or to show young people coming in where there would be free housing and where people could go to stay overnight.

So he outlined some of the organizational plans that the Yippies in Chicago, that he had been cooperating with, had tried to put together to keep some peace and to keep some orderliness about the gathering.

Q Does that complete your recollection of Mr. Hoffman's conversation with you?

A Yes.

Q Now, do you recall whether or not Mr. Hoffman mentioned to you at that time the status of the rock groups that were coming to Chicago in light of the permit negotiations?

MR. FORAN: Objection.

THE COURT: I sustain the objection.

BY MR. WEINGLASS:

Q Having exhausted your recollection, do you recall whether or not Mr. Hoffman mentioned anything about the rock band groups at that time?

A Yes, he did.

MR. FORAN: Objection.

THE COURT: I sustain the objection.

MR. WEINGLASS: May I have the basis for the objection and for the Court's ruling?

MR. FORAN: Your Honor, he is not relating a part of his own state of mind or a part of his plan. That is the only exception to the hearsay rule.

MR. WEINGLASS: It is not hearsay. It is a conversation by the defendant to the witness, and the witness is permitted to relate that. It is relevant, since we already have had substantial testimony in this case about the relationship between the City of Chicago's unwillingness to grant the permit and how that affected the defendants' plans for going ahead with the Festival of Life.

THE COURT: I will let my ruling stand.

BY MR. WEINGLASS:

Q On August 24, 1968, directing your attention to the morning of August 24, 1968, where were you?

A I was on a plane coming from New York to Chicago.

Q Were you flying alone or were you in the company of other people?

A I flew alone.

Q Now, enroute to Chicago while you were on the plane, what if anything did you do?

A I wrote poetry, wrote out a statement of what I thought was going on in Chicago at the time.

Q And where did you write that poem?

A On the airplane.

Q Did you write on any particular piece of paper or pad?

A I wrote it in a record journal notebook that I keep for composing poetry and for writing down what is going on in my head.

Q That is your daily journal?

A Whenever I have any idea to write down, yes. Every other day more likely.

MR. WEINGLASS: If the Court please, the daily journal which the witness is referring to has been marked D-152 for identification.

(The said document was thereupon marked Defendants' Exhibit 152 for identification.)

BY MR. WEINGLASS:

Q Did you write that poem in that daily journal?

A Yes, sir.

Q And is that daily journal now before you?

A Yes, here.

Q Is it written in your handwriting or someone else's own handwriting?

A My own handwriting.

Q And did you preserve that document in its present condition?

A Yes, sir.

Q Is the document in the same condition today as it was the day that you wrote the poem?

A Exactly the same.

Q I am excluding subsequent entries in your journal.

A Right.

Q Now, may I please have that?

A Yes.

MR. WEINGLASS: I am showing that portion of D-152 pertaining to the poem that was written by this witness on that day --

THE COURT: What was the date?

MR. WEINGLASS: August 24. -- and giving the Government an opportunity to examine that document.

I shall offer that document into evidence and only that portion of the document dealing with this particular poem as Defense Exhibit 152.

MR. FORAN: Objection.

THE COURT: You object?

MR. FORAN: I object. This man is not on trial.

THE COURT: I will look at it. Mr. Marshal.

(Defendants' Exhibit 152 for identification was handed to the Court.)

THE COURT: I sustain the objection to Defendants' Exhibit No. 152 for identification.

BY MR. WEINGLASS:

Q Do you recall what time of day you arrived in the City of Chicago on the 24th of August?

A Around 2:00 o'clock or so, mid-day, 3:00 o'clock.

Q Do you recall where you were on that day at 4:00 p.m.?

A Yes.

Q Where were you?

A I went to a meeting at the free theatre across the street from the Lincoln Park.

Q Who was there?

A Abbie Hoffman, Jerry Rubin, Ed Sanders, Stew Albert, and many other people whom I didn't know, people who were working on the Youth International Party festival.

Q Was Paul Krassner there?

A Yes.

Q Keith Lampe?

A Yes, Keith Lampe.

Q Was David Stein there?

MR. FORAN: I object, your Honor.

THE COURT: I sustain the objection.

MR. FORAN: It is leading and suggestive.

THE COURT: I sustain the objection.

MR. WEINGLASS: That was a preliminary question.

BY MR. WEINGLASS:

Q Does that exhaust your recollection as to who was there?

A That is my recollection of names.

Q Was David Stein there?

A I don't know him, I don't think.

Q Did you hear the defendant, Jerry Rubin, say anything at this meeting?

A Yes.

Q Will you relate to the Court and jury what Jerry Rubin said?

A Jerry Rubin said that he didn't think the police would attack the kids who were in the park at night if there were enough kids there, that he didn't think it would be a good thing to fight over the park if the police started fighting with the kids, if the police attacked the kids and tried to drive them out of the park as the police had announced at 11:00 o'clock, that as far as he was concerned, he wanted to leave the park at 9:00 and would not encourage anybody to fight and get hurt that evening if the police did physically try to force everybody out of the park. That was on Saturday night, the first night when people would be in the park.

Q Did the defendant, Abbie Hoffman, say anything at this meeting?

A Abbie Hoffman said the park wasn't worth fighting for, that we had on our responsibility invited many thousands of kids to Chicago for a happy festival of life, for an alternative proposition to the festival of death that the politicians were putting on, and that it wasn't right to lead them or encourage them to get into a violent argument with the police over staying in the park overnight. He didn't know, he said he didn't know what to say to those who wanted to stay and fight for what they felt was their liberty, but he wasn't going to encourage anybody to fight, and he was going to leave when forced himself.

Q Was there then a discussion following these two speeches?

A Yes.

Q And was an agreement reached between the persons present as to a policy with respect to staying in the park?

MR. FORAN: I object. Leading and suggestive.

THE COURT: I sustain the objection to the question.

MR. WEINGLASS: Your Honor, we followed the practice in the courtroom up to this point to allow a question --

THE COURT: You always go back in history. I am only passing on one question. The form of the question is clearly bad.

MR. WEINGLASS: Am I not to be allowed --

THE COURT: Whether or not there was an agreement is not a good question, under the matter of the law of evidence.

BY MR. WEINGLASS:

Q At approximately 10:30 that night, where were you?

A I was in Lincoln Park.

Q And what occurred in Lincoln Park at approximately 10:30, if you can recall?

A I had come in with Jean Genet. No, Ed Sanders, I had come in with Ed Sanders into the park, talking with Ed Sanders, asking him if the individual statements --

MR. FORAN: Objection, your Honor.

THE COURT: I sustain the objection, and strike the words "talking with Sanders," and what followed. I direct the jury to disregard them.

BY MR. WEINGLASS:

Q When you came to the park with Ed Sanders, what did you see in the park at that time as you entered the park?

A There were several thousand young people gathered, waiting, late at night. It was dark. There were some bonfires burning in trash cans. Everybody was standing around not knowing what to do.

MR. FORAN: Objection, your Honor.

THE COURT: "Standing around, not knowing what to do," those words may go out, and the jury is directed to disregard them.

BY MR. WEINGLASS:

Q Now, do you recall what, if anything, occurred at 10:30?

A There was a sudden burst of lights in the center of the park, and a group of policemen moved in fast to where the bonfires were and kicked over the bonfires.

Q Then what --

A There was a great deal of consternation and movement and shouting among the crowd in the park, and I turned, surprised, because it was early. The police were or had given 11:00 o'clock as the date or as the time --

MR. FORAN: Objection, your Honor.

THE COURT: Yes, "I was surprised," and the words which follow may go out. The jury is directed to disregard them.

BY MR. WEINGLASS:

Q When you observed the police doing this what, if anything, did you do?

A I turned to Sanders and said, "They are not supposed to be here until 11:00."

MR. FORAN: Objection.

THE COURT: I sustain the objection.

BY MR. WEINGLASS:

Q Without relating what you said to another person, Mr. Ginsberg, what did you do at the time you saw the police do this?

A I started the chant, O-o-m-m-m-m-m-m, O-o-m-m-m-m-m-m.

MR. FORAN: All right, we have had a demonstration.

THE COURT: All right.

MR. FORAN: From here on, I object.

THE COURT: You haven't said that you objected.

MR. FORAN: I do after the second one.

THE COURT: After two of them? I sustain the objection.

MR. WEINGLASS: If the Court please, there has been much testimony by the Government's witnesses as to this Om technique which was used in the park. Are we only going to hear whether there were stones or people throwing things, or shouting things, or using obscenities? Why do we draw the line here? Why can't we also hear what is being said in the area of calming the crowd?

MR. FORAN: I have no objection to the two Om's that we have had. However, I just didn't want it to go on all morning.

THE COURT: The two, however you characterize what the witness did, may remain of record, and he may not continue in the same vein.

BY MR. WEINGLASS:

Q Did you finish your answer?

A I am afraid I will be in contempt if I continue to Om. We walked out of the park.

Q How long did you --

A We walked out of the park. We continued chanting the Om for at least twenty minutes, slowly, gathering other people, chanting, Ed Sanders and I in the center, until there were a group maybe of 15 or 20 making a very solid heavy vibrational change of aim that penetrated the immediate area around us, and attracted other people, and so we walked out slowly toward the street, toward the Lincoln Park Hotel.

Q Now, will you explain to the Court and jury what the chant Om is?

MR. FORAN: I object to that.

THE COURT: I sustain the objection.

BY MR. WEINGLASS:

Q What is the purpose of the chant Om?

MR. FORAN: Objection.

THE COURT: I sustain the objection.

MR. WEINGLASS: Your Honor, why is the jury not being permitted to gain an understanding of this technique which is a technique used to control and quiet a crowd? We haven't objected to their testifying about stoning police cars and using obscenities. Now why are we being precluded from putting our defense in that there was an attempt on the part of this witness to calm and quiet the crowd? I don't know why we are not being permitted by the Court --

THE COURT: The statement by Mr. Weinglass that the defense is being precluded from putting its defense in may go out and the jury is directed to disregard it. There have been several witnesses for the defense who have testified and this witness is a defense witness. He is testifying. The Court has ruled on one question, was obligated to rule on one question. It seems that every time there is an adverse ruling you get the impression or try to give the impression, Mr. Weinglass, that the Court is ruling unfairly. I am doing my best to rule according to the rules of evidence.

MR. WEINGLASS: Well, your Honor, I am not --

THE COURT: That is my ruling, sir.

MR. WEINGLASS: I am not trying to give an impression --

THE COURT: That is my ruling and I ask you to continue your direct examination.

MR. WEINGLASS: The Government witnesses were permitted to testify about the purpose of Wash Oi, snake dancing, karate; now why can't our witness testify about the purpose of Om and other techniques which were intended to quiet the crowd.

MR. FORAN: Of course, your Honor, the Government never did testify to purposes. We testified to what was done in the park. We have no objection to this witness testifying to what he saw done or what he did himself, but I object to him talking about purposes and I ask your Honor that you direct the jury to disregard the statements of Mr. Weinglass.

THE COURT: I have already done so.

MR. WEINGLASS: If Mr. Foran would represent to this court that his witnesses never said the purpose of snake dancing was to break through police lines, I will withdraw my objection.

MR. FORAN: Your Honor, the defendants told the purpose in the park.

THE COURT: I will direct you, sir, to continue with the direct examination of this witness if you have any additional questions.

BY MR. WEINGLASS:

Q How long did the Om continue, Mr. Ginsberg?

MR. FORAN: Objection, your Honor, as asked and answered.

THE COURT: If the witness can remember --

MR. FORAN: Your Honor --

THE COURT: I will let him answer.

MR. FORAN: Your Honor, he said 20 minutes. He already testified.

THE COURT: I know, but if he can remember that he answered, I will let him repeat it.

THE WITNESS: Yes. About 20 minutes, perhaps longer.

THE COURT: It merely demonstrates that you asked the same question twice. I will let the second answer stand.

BY MR. WEINGLASS:

Q Now what could you observe was the condition of the people in the park at the time you began your Om chant?

A A great deal of swift and agitated motion in many different directions without any center and without any calm.

When we began chanting, as it included more and more people, there was one central sound and one central rhythmic behavior vocalized by all the people who participated and a slow quietening of the physical behavior of the people that were slowly moving out of the park. They all moved in one direction, those who were involved in the chanting, out of the park and away from the police calmly without running and without physically agitated behavior.

Q At the end of your Om chant, where were you and the crowd?

MR. FORAN: I object to that, your Honor. We didn't have any testimony about a crowd.

THE COURT: I didn't hear that.

MR. FORAN: We had 15 or 20 people participating in this thing.

MR. WEINGLASS: I will withdraw that question.

MR. FORAN: Now we have a crowd.

BY MR. WEINGLASS:

Q At the end of the Om chant, how many people were in your immediate vicinity?

A I remember at least a hundred.

Q Where was that group located at the end of your Om chant?

A That group as well as most of the people in the park arrived outside at the end of the park on the street that borders the park across from the Lincoln Park Hotel.

Q Where did you go after that?

A I wandered up and down the street and then went to my hotel.

Q Now directing your attention to the next day which is Sunday, August 25th, where were you in the morning that day?

A Downtown to the Hilton Hotel, Grant Park and the Hilton Hotel, wandering around.

Q Did you have occasion while you were downtown near the Hilton Hotel to go into the hotel?

A Yes.

Q When you got into the hotel, who, if anyone, did you meet?

A I met David Dellinger.

Q Was Mr. Dellinger alone?

A No, I met him with -- I think when I met him he was alone, yes.

Q And did you and Mr. Dellinger subsequently meet another person?

A Yes, we went in and had coffee with Mr. Baugher of City Hall.

Q Could you indicate to the court and jury what conversation occurred in the presence of Mr. Dellinger while you were seated with Mr. Dellinger and Mr. Baugher?

MR. FORAN: Your Honor, may we have who was present? May we have a statement by the witness who was present?

THE COURT: He said Mr. Dellinger and Mr. Baugher and himself.
Did you not, Mr. Witness?

THE WITNESS: Yes, sir.

THE COURT: Those three persons, only those three persons were present, is that right?

THE WITNESS: As I remember, that is all there were.

BY MR. WEINGLASS:

Q Now what conversation in the presence of Mr. Dellinger ensued at that meeting?

A I believe that Mr. Baugher congratulated me on chanting Om and keeping the situation in the park peaceful.

Q And did you say anything in response to that?

A I said that if the city would grant a permit, then it would insure that there would be peace in the march because then there would be no conflict between the police and the kids who had come to Chicago for the Festival of Life and to observe the convention, and that it would be wise of the city even if it didn't grant a permit for the meetings in the park to at least grant a permit for a loud speaker system so that we could get on the loud speaker system and keep control of the crowd, large crowds of people, by chanting and by direction, so it wouldn't turn into an anarchic situation where people were running around like chickens with their heads off facing the police, not knowing what the police were going to do. If he would intervene with City Hall to see if we had a loud speaker system, it might insure more calm and more peace within the park.

Q What did Mr. Baugher say about that?

A He thought it was a good idea and he would talk to the people at City Hall and talk to Mr. Stahl and see where he could get a loud speaker for that afternoon when a rock festival was being planned.

Q Do you know, Mr. Ginsberg, whether Mr. Baugher actually did get a loud speaker?

MR. FORAN: Objection.

THE COURT: I sustain the objection.

BY MR. WEINGLASS:

Q Now at approximately three o'clock that afternoon which was Sunday, where were you?

A By the loud speaker in the center of the park where there was the MC5, a Detroit rock group led by John Sinclair who was at the microphone, so I came up to John Sinclair who had been arranging the music part of the day and asked him if I could do a bit of chanting on the microphone.

Q And what occurred at that time?

A I was introduced on the microphone and for about fifteen minutes chanted the Hare Krishna Mantra with the harmonium and then chanted a poem of William Blake in order to calm the crowd and to advise those who were of a violent nature --

MR. FORAN: Objection, your Honor.

THE COURT: I sustain the objection. The reference of the witness to his having spoken or chanted a poem of William Blake may go out and the jury is directed to disregard it.

BY MR. WEINGLASS:

Q Could you just state without chanting the poem of William Blake to the jury?

A "'I die, I die!', the Mother said,
'My Children die for lack of Bread.
What more has the merciless Tyrant said?'
The Monk sat down on the Stony Bed.

"The blood red ran from the Grey Monk's side,
His hands & feet were wounded wide,
His Body bent, his arms & knees
Like to the roots of ancient trees.

"His eye was dry; no tear could flow;
A hollow groan first spoke his woe.
He trembled & shudder'd upon the Bed;
At length with a feeble cry he said:

"When God commanded this hand to write
In the studious hours of deep midnight,
He told me the writing I wrote should prove
The Bane of all that on Earth I lov'd.

"My Brother starv'd between two Walls,
His children's Cry my Soul appalls;
I mock'd at the wrack & griding chain,
My bent body mocks their torturing pain.

"Thy Father drew his sword in the North,
With his thousands strong he marched forth;
Thy Brother has arm'd himself in Steel
To avenge the wrongs thy Children feel.

"But vain the Sword & vain the Bow,
They never can work War's overthrow.
The Hermit's Prayer & the Widow's tear
Alone can free the World from fear.

"For a Tear is an Intellectual Thing,
And a Sigh is the Sword of an Angel King,
And the bitter groan of the Martyr's woe
Is an Arrow from the Almightie's Bow.

"The hand of Vengeance found the Bed
To which the Purple Tyrant fled;
The iron hand crush'd the Tyrant's head
And became a Tyrant in his stead."

Q Did you remain in the park after that?

A Yes.

Q How long did you remain in the park?

A I was in the park until about 11:30 that night.

Q Now from this time until the time you left the park, did you have occasion to see the defendant Jerry Rubin in the park?

A No.

Q What, if anything, did you do for the remainder of the time that you were in the park?

A First I walked around away from the loud speaker system and the rock and roll music that was going on to the center of the park where suddenly a group of policemen appeared in the middle of the younger people. There was an appearance of a great mass of policemen going through the center of the park. I was afraid then, thinking they were going to make trouble --

MR. FORAN: Objection to his state of mind.

THE COURT: "I was afraid then --"

THE WITNESS: Adrenalin ran in my body.

THE COURT: "I was afraid then" and all the words that followed may go out and the jury is directed to disregard them.

BY MR. WEINGLASS:

Q What did you do when you saw the policemen in the center of the crowd?

A Adrenalin ran through my body. I sat down on a green hillside with a group of younger people that were walking with me at about 3:30 in the afternoon, 4:00 o'clock, sat, crossed my legs and began chanting O-o-m -- O-o-m-m-m, O-o-m-m-m, O-o-m-m-m.

MR. FORAN: I gave him four that time.

THE WITNESS: I continued chanting for seven hours.

MR. WEINGLASS: I am sorry, I did not hear the answer.

THE COURT: He said he continued chanting for seven hours. Seven hours, was it, sir?

THE WITNESS: Until 10:30.

THE COURT: I wanted to know what your answer was. Did you say you continued chanting for seven hours?

THE WITNESS: Seven hours, yes.

THE COURT: I wanted Mr. Weinglass to have your answer. He didn't hear you.

THE WITNESS: About six hours I chanted Om and for the seventh hour concluded with the chant Hare Krishna, Hare Krishna, Krishna, Krishna, Hare, Hare, Hare Rama, Hare Rama, Rama Rama, Hare, Hare.

BY MR. WEINGLASS:

Q When you chanted during this period of time, were you joined in the chant?

A Yes, many people joined me. We formed a single -- there were groups -- it was a long period of time, the group shrank and increased as the day went on. Toward dusk there must have been -- there were about 100, 200 people, shrinking, people coming and joining and going around, but there was a permanent group that stayed with me of about 50 people who continued chanting in unison.

Q Now directing your attention to Monday night, that is August 26, at approximately 11:30 in the evening, where were you?

A I had finished chanting and went down to talk to a police official who was in the center of a gathering of police at the side of the park.

Q In what park were you?

A Lincoln Park.

Q This is approximately what time of night?

A Around 11:00.

Q Now was there any kind of physical obstruction in the park on Monday night at that time?

A I went to talk to the police a little earlier than 11:00. At 11:00 I was by a barricade that was set up, a pile of trash cans and police barricades, wooden horses, I believe.

Q As you got there, what was occurring at that barricade?

A There were a lot of young kids, some black, some white, shouting and beating on the tin barrels, making a fearsome noise.

Q What did you do after you got there?

A Started chanting Om there.

Q And were you joined in that chant?

A For a while I was joined in the chant by a lot of other people who were there until the chant encompassed most of the people by the barricade and we raised a huge loud sustained series of Oms into the air loud enough to like include everybody.

Q Now did anything occur that caused that process to stop?

A We were in the midst --

MR. FORAN: Objection, your Honor.

THE COURT: I sustain the objection.

BY MR. WEINGLASS:

Q How long was the group that was there chanting as you just indicated?

A About fifteen minutes.

Q Then what happened.

A Just as it reached like a great unison crescendo when all of a sudden a police car came rolling down into the group, right into the center of the group where I was standing, and with a lot of crashing and tinkling sound of glass and broke up the chanting, broke up the unison and the physical -- everybody was holding onto each other physically -- broke up that physical community that had been built and broke up the sound chant that had been built.

Q Did this police car approach from the opposite side of that barrier or did they approach from the crowd side of the barrier?

A They came from behind the crowd.

Q And did you notice as you were standing there what, if anything, the crowd did with respect to that police car?

A People screamed, people stopped chanting, some people fled. I moved back. There was a crash of glass.

Q When you moved back, what did you do?

A I started chanting Om again.

Q Were you joined in your chant?

A Yes.

Q What occurred at that time?

A I started moving away from the scene. I started moving away from the scene because there was violence there.

Q When you say there was violence there, will you describe what you mean?

A The police car had come, had crashed right into the crowd.

Q And how long did you stay in that area after the police car came into the crowd?

A I started moving out immediately.

Q Now directing your attention to Tuesday afternoon, where were you the next day which was August 27?

A I was in Lincoln Park.

Q O.K.

MR. WEINGLASS: I am sorry, I will withdraw that question. I did get a little bit ahead.

THE COURT: Do you want the answer stricken?

MR. WEINGLASS: Yes.

THE COURT: All right. Leave to withdraw the question, and the answer will be stricken and the jury is directed to disregard the answer.

BY MR. WEINGLASS:

Q Mr. Ginsberg, I show you a document marked D-153 for identification, and ask you whether or not you can identify that document.

A Yes, it is a press release poem that was composed by myself and Ed Sanders, and circulated through the Yippie underground media immediately preceding the convention and printed in the underground number, "Rat, Subterranean News," which was circulated in Lincoln Park.

Q Who wrote that press release?

A I did.

Q Who printed it and published it?

A It was printed by "Rat," which is a New York City underground newspaper that printed a convention special issue and brought thousands of copies to Chicago to circulate in the park.

Q Do you recall when that was printed and circulated?

A It was printed and circulated several days before the convention, before the 24th. When I arrived in Chicago on the 24th, I found it in Chicago.

MR. WEINGLASS: Your Honor, at this point, the defense offers into evidence as D-153 a document previously marked as D-153 for identification, and the document is being handed to the prosecution for examination.

MR. FORAN: I object, your Honor.

THE COURT: You object to it?

MR. FORAN: Yes, your Honor.

THE COURT: May I see it, Mr. Marshal, please.

(Defendants' Exhibit D-153 for identification was handed to the Court.)

MR. FORAN: Your Honor, it has nothing to do with these defendants or with this case.

THE COURT: I sustain the objection.
The objection of the Government to Defendants' Exhibit 153 for identification will be sustained.

MR. WEINGLASS: Your Honor, if you Honor please, we have no evidence to show peaceful intent.

THE COURT: You are fond of asking questions as though my rulings are all unfair. I am sustaining the objection, sir, because the document is totally irrelevant and immaterial, and does not contribute anything to resolving the issues presented by the indictment here and the pleas of not guilty. You may ask another question.

MR. WEINGLASS: Your Honor admitted in this case once before a police file --

THE COURT: You may ask another question. There has been a ruling on that exhibit. If you have another question now, you may put it to the witness.

BY MR. WEINGLASS:

Q Mr. Ginsberg, I got a little ahead of myself. Going back to early, very early in the morning, about six a.m. on Tuesday, where were you?

A I was on the beach at the lake front at Lincoln Park, conducting a Mantra chanting ceremony that had been arranged to be performed by Abbie Hoffman and Jerry Rubin and the other people who were planning the weekly schedule of Yippy activities.

Q Now, this ritual or ceremony, was it attended by many persons?

A Yes, Abbie Hoffman came, plus a number of other young people.

Q What occurred at this ritual?

A We got together to greet the morning with Tibetan Buddhist magic-prayer formulas, mantras, beginning with Om Raksa, Raksa, Hum, Hum, Hum, Phat, Svaha, the mantra to purify a site for the ceremony.
We chanted in Muslim Sufi, Arab Mantra, La Illaha Ill Allah Who. We chanted Om. We chanted Hare Krishna Hare --
H-a-r-e, K-r-i-s-h-n-a, H-a-r-e. Shall I spell the others, sir?

THE COURT: Just answer the questions of the lawyer.

THE WITNESS: With Abbie Hoffman and others, I continued the chanting for several hours.

BY MR. WEINGLASS:

Q Now, where was Abbie Hoffman seated?

A He was seated on my left, very close.

Q And what was he doing during this ceremony, if anything?

A Meditating and chanting.

Q How long did this ceremony last?

A Well, it was shorter than intended. Abbie had arranged it for dawn, but I came a little late, so it went on for about two hours.

Q Now, on Tuesday afternoon that same day, where were you?

A I was in the center of Lincoln Park.

Q What were you doing?

A We had re-scheduled the Mantra chanting session at Abbie Hoffman's request so that we would get more people involved in it, and I was sitting on a carpet in the center of the park, in the center of a circle with a group of other people, some of whom were trained in Mantra chanting, and we chanted for several hours again.

Q I show you two photographs marked respectively D-154 for identification and 155, and ask you if you can identify both of those photographs.

A Yes, they were taken on that Tuesday afternoon in the center of that Mantra chanting crowd.

Q Do those photographs accurately and truly portray yourself and the people around you at that time?

A There were more people later on, than the photograph indicates.

Q Does this photograph portray the group at any particular time?

A I think early in the afternoon when we were beginning. It is an accurate photo of the center of the group.

MR. WEINGLASS: At this time, the defense offers D-154 and 155 for identification as D-154 and D-155, as Defendants' Exhibits.

MR. FORAN: No objection.

THE COURT: With no objection, Defendants' Exhibits 154 and 155 respectively for identification, may be admitted into evidence as Defendants' exhibits bearing the numbers indicated.

(Whereupon said exhibits, being so offered and received in evidence, were marked Defendants' Exhibits 154 and 155 in evidence.)

BY MR. WEINGLASS:

Q How long did the chanting session continue?

A Several hours.

Q Now, at approximately 8:00 p.m. that evening, where were you? This is Tuesday night, August 27.

A I came with a party of writers to the un-birthday party of President Johnson at the Coliseum in Chicago.

Q Who was with you?

A The French writer, Jean Genet, poet-novelist. The American novelist, William Seward (W.S.) Burroughs, the novelist.
The novelist, Terry Southern, who had written "Doctor Strangelove."
An editor from Esquire, John Berendt, B-e-r-e-n-d-t.
Richard Seaver, editor of Grove Press, New York, a publishing company. Myself. We all went together.

Q And approximately what time did you arrive?

A Eight, 8:30.

Q Now, when you arrived at the Coliseum, did you see any of the defendants present?

A Yes.

Q Who, if anyone, did you see?

A Abbie Hoffman.

Q Where was he?

A He was seated several rows down from our party behind the stage.

Q Did you talk to him at that time?

A Yes, I want --

Q Will you relate to the Court and jury what occurred when you talked to him?

A I went down and sat next to him and kissed him, and then pointed back up at Jean Genet, who was there, and told Abbie that Genet was there, and signalled to Genet so they would see each other because they had met previously.

Q Did you subsequently perform at the Coliseum?

A I had lost my voice chanting the day before and that afternoon, so my larynx was reduced to croaking, so I had written a statement about the improprieties of police behavior which was read aloud at the Coliseum along with statements by Mr. Genet and Mr. Burroughs, but the statement was read for me by Ed Sanders while I sat on the stage in Buddhist meditation Asana, posture.

Q I show you two photographs marked 156 and 157. I ask you to examine those photographs. Do you recognize those photographs?

A Yes.

Q What do they depict?

A They depict the position that I was sitting in on the stage, in Buddhist zazen meditation, Buddhist posture, Soto Zen, while Ed Sanders behind me was reading my statement.

MR. WEINGLASS: If your Honor please, we offer into evidence D-156 and D-157 as Defendants' Exhibits D-156 and D-157. The exhibits have been handed to the prosecution for examination.

MR. FORAN: No objection.

THE COURT: With no objection, Defendants' Exhibits 156 and 157 respectively for identification may be admitted into evidence as Defendants' Exhibits bearing the indicated numbers.

(The said exhibits, so offered and received in evidence, were marked Defendants' Exhibits 156 and 157.)

BY MR. WEINGLASS:

Q Now, on stage that evening, did you see any of the other defendants in this case?

A I don't remember.

Q Approximately what time did you leave the Coliseum that night?

A Around 9:30.

Q Did you hear the defendant, Abbie Hoffman, speak at the Coliseum that night?

A I saw him speaking, but I didn't listen.

Q Now, when you left the Coliseum, where, if anywhere, did you go?

A The group I was with, Mr. Genet, Mr. Burroughs and Mr. Seaver and Terry Southern, all went back to Lincoln Park.

Q What time did you arrive in the park?

A Eleven, 11:30.

Q What was occurring at the park as you got there?

A There was a great crowd lining the outskirts of the park and a little way into the park on the inner roads, and there was a larger crowd moving in toward the center. We all moved in toward the center and at the center of the park, there was a group of ministers and rabbis who had elevated a great cross about ten-foot high in the middle of a circle of people who were sitting around, quietly, listening to the ministers conduct a ceremony.

Q How many people were there?

A It must have been about a thousand.

Q Were you there while the ceremony was being conducted?

A Yes.

Q And would you relate to the court and the jury what was being said and done at that time?

A The ministers were telling whoever wanted to participate in the ceremony to sit down and be quiet, and when singing was done, to sing in unison. There were a few people who were making more disturbing noises. The ministers were trying to calm them down and have them sit down. Everybody was seated around the cross which was at the center of hundreds of people, people right around the very center adjoining the cross. Everybody was singing, "We shall overcome," and "Onward

Christian Soldiers," I believe. They were old hymn tunes.

Q After the service was over, what if anything occurred at that place?

A The cross was lifted up. At the other side behind the circle that we were observing as we were seated -- I was seated with my friends on a little hillock looking down on the crowd which had the cross in the center -- and on the other side, there were a lot of glarey lights hundreds of feet away down the field. The ministers lifted up the cross and took it to the edge of the crowd and set it down facing the lights where the police were. In other words, they confronted the police lines with the Cross of Christ.

Q Where were you at the time that that occurred?

A I stayed sitting on the hill, watching the scene below me.

Q Could you see this?

A Yes.

Q And after the ministers moved the cross to another location which you have indicated, what happened?

A After, I don't know, a short period of time, there was a burst of smoke and tear gas around the cross, and the cross was enveloped with tear gas, and the people who were carrying the cross were enveloped with tear gas which began slowly drifting over the crowd.

Q Now prior to that happening, did you hear any announcement on any type of speaker equipment?

A No, none at all.

Q Were you told to get out of the park?

A I heard no announcement saying to get out of the park, no.

Q And when you saw the persons with the cross and the cross being gassed, what if anything did you do?

A I turned to Burroughs and said, "They have gassed the cross of Christ."

MR. FORAN: Objection, if the Court please. I ask that the answer be stricken.

BY MR. WEINGLASS:

Q Without relating what you said, Mr. Ginsberg, what did you do at that time?

A I took Bill Burroughs' hand and took Terry Southern's hand, and we turned from the cross which was covered with gas in the glarey lights that were coming from the police-lights that were shining through the tear gas on the cross - and walked slowly out of the park.

Q On Wednesday, the next day, at approximately 3:45 in the afternoon, do you recall where you were?

A Yes.

Q Where were you?

A Entering the Grant Park bandshell area, where there was a Mobilization meeting or rally going on.

Q Did you enter the area alone or were you with other people?

A No, I was still with the same group of literary fellows, poets and writers.

Q Where did you go in the bandshell area?

A We had started out but couldn't get there early because all the entrances to that area, overpasses, were blocked off by policemen saying that we couldn't enter. So we had to go all the way down south to the bottom of the park and enter over a wooden trestle. So when we entered, we all went and sat down in the center of the crowd, waiting, watching.

Q And did you at any time later get up to the bandshell stage?

A Yes. I walked up to the apron or front of the stage and saw David Dellinger and told him that I was there and that Burroughs was there and Jean Genet was there and that they were all willing to be present and testify to the righteousness of the occasion and that we would like to be on the stage.

Q Were you then invited onto the stage?

A He said, "By all means invite them on."

Q Were you then introduced?

A Yes.

Q Who introduced you, do you recall?

A I believe Mr. Dellinger.

Q Was Mr. Burroughs introduced?

A Yes.

Q Any other person who was with you?

A Yes. Jean Genet was also introduced.

Q Did you speak?

A I croaked, yes.

THE COURT: What was that last? You say you what?

THE WITNESS: I croaked. My voice was gone. I chanted or tried to chant.

BY MR. WEINGLASS:

Q Which chant did you chant at this time?

A Om.

Q Now after the rally was over, did you remain for the rest of the rally?

A Yes. I was in the back of the stage talking with Mr. Burroughs and Mr. Genet.

Q Did you hear the speakers that followed?

A I didn't pay much attention to most of them. There was one that I heard.

Q Do you recall who that was?

A Louis Abolafia, whom I knew from New York.

Q And who is he?

A Kind of a Bohemian trickster, street theatre candidate for president. He had announced his candidacy for president a number of times and his campaign slogan was, "I have nothing to hide," and he showed himself in a photograph with his hand over his lap, but otherwise naked.

Q Do you recall when in the course of the rally you heard Mr. Abolafia speak?

A Oh, I think toward the end of the rally before the formation of the parade.

Q Was he introduced?

A No, he just appeared from nowhere and got up to the microphone and started yelling into it.

Q Do you recall hearing what he was yelling?

A "The police out there are armed and violent. You are walking into a death trap."

Q When you heard him yelling that over the microphone, what, if anything, did you do?

A I went down and sat next to him and grabbed his leg and started tickling him and said, "Hare Krishna, Louis."

While he was talking, I sat down next to him while he was talking and tried to calm him down and distract him a little bit by tickling him.

Q Now when the rally was over, did you have occasion to talk with Mr. Dellinger?

A Yes. I went down off the platform into the crowd that was forming for the peace march then and saw Mr. Dellinger.

Q And what did Mr. Dellinger say to you at that time?

A He looked me in the eye, took my arm and said, "Allen, will you please march up front in the front line with me?"

Q And what did you say to him?

A I said, "Well, I am here with Burroughs and Genet and Terry Southern," and he said, "Well, all of you together, can you form a front line and be sure to stay behind me in the front line, be the first of the group of marchers?"

Q And did you form such a line?

A Yes. I went and told Burroughs and Genet and they all agreed and we went right up front.

Q Who was in front of you, immediately in front of you?

A Immediately in front was one fellow carrying on his head a portable loud speaker equipment, Mr. Dellinger, and immediately behind him a group of marshals and then ourselves as the head of the line of peace-manifesting marchers.

Q How were you walking?

A Slowly.

Q Were your arms --

A Our arms were all linked together and we were carrying flowers. Someone had brought flowers up to the back of the stage and so we distributed them around to the first rows of marchers so all of the marchers had flowers.

Q Now how far did you walk?

A We were still in the park. It was like a couple of blocks within the park along the side of a viaduct.

Q After you walked the several blocks, what occurred?

A We came to a halt in front of a large guard of armed human beings in uniform who were blocking our way, people with machine guns, jeeps, I believe, police, and what looked to me like soldiers on our side and in front of us.

Q And what happened at that point?

A Mr. Dellinger -- the march stopped and we waited not quite knowing what to do. I heard -- all along I had heard Dave Dellinger saying, "This is a peaceful march. All those who want to participate in a peaceful march please join our line. All those who are not peaceful, please go away and don't join our line."

He continued that up to the point when we were stopped.

Q When you were stopped, did you see what Dellinger did at that time?

A He went forward to talk to the police heads that were there.

Q Did you go over with him or did you remain behind?

A Yes, I went over with him, took his arm for one moment and also brought a little armful of flowers that had been given us as we left the bandshell.

Q And what did you do with the flowers, if anything?

A Mr. Dellinger and the city agents, city officials and police heads were talking together, negotiating, and whenever they seemed to me to be agitated, I took the flowers and put them in between their faces and shook them around a little which made Mr. Elrod smile, I remember.

Q Do you know who Mr. Elrod is?

A He was the chief Corporation Counsel or the chief lawyer of the city, I believe.

Q Now did you return to the line that you had left to go up with Mr. Dellinger at any point in time?

A Yes. There was a time when there was a long wait for messages to be sent back and forth. Mr. Dellinger told me would I please go to the loud speaker system and the portable microphone and the bull horn that was being carried on the head of the kid, would I get up to the microphone and calm the crowd and calm the police by chanting because there was this long line behind us, there was a great mass of armed people in front of us, it was a tricky, scary moment. So

Dave Dellinger asked me to get up on the microphone and begin chanting and chant as long as I pleased and chant as deeply as I pleased.

Q Did you do that?

A Yes.

Q Did anyone join you in chanting?

A Yes, many people.

Q At that point where were the people, standing or seated?

A They were mostly seated. Everybody had sat down for the long wait as we were blocked, so everybody was seated, some cross-legged on the ground. I was standing facing the crowd lined up to march.

Q Now do you recall how long the crowd remained in that condition?

A Continuously, like it remained seated as long as I was chanting Om Sri Maitreya, which was the chant --

Q Can you estimate in terms of time, minutes or hours, how long that condition lasted?

A The chanting and quiet, calm?

Q Yes.

A Fifteen minutes, I believe.

Q And after the chanting stopped, what occurred?

A Everything was very quiet, still.

Q And how long did that condition last?

A Another 20 minutes.

Q Now did there come a time when you left this area?

A Much later, yes. I stayed sitting there. There were other moves and other movements between the police and Mr. Dellinger and the line of march.

Q How long did you remain there?

A About three-quarters of an hour.

Q At the end of that three-quarters of an hour, what, if anything, did you do?

A I got up to walk away with Mr. Dellinger from the march. I think Mr. Dellinger announced that the march was over and had been victorious inasmuch as the Government had simply forced us to abandon our citizen's right to have a peaceful assembly for redress of grievances and there was nothing we could do about it at that point. We had offered ourselves to be arrested and were not being arrested and so we were going to disperse and move on. Mr. Dellinger declared the march over and so we began dispersing.

Q And when you left, did you leave alone?

A I left with Mr. Dellinger.

Q Was anyone else in your presence?

A There was a kid carrying the microphone and the loud speaker and many people -- I mean, it was like a large group, a loosely-knit group of people moving around, not quite knowing where to go actually.

Q Where did you go when you left?

A I started walking north past the bridges but I wanted to get out onto Michigan Avenue by the hotels but couldn't because all of the bridges were blocked with soldiers. So I kept going further and further north until I ran into tear gas. There was tear gas on the street -- in the park, even though like nothing was happening, and people were just trying to get out. I was blocked and couldn't leave, couldn't leave the area, couldn't leave Grant Park, and continued walking north, lost Mr. Dellinger --

MR. FORAN: Objection, your Honor, as going far afield.

THE COURT: I sustain the objection.
"I was blocked and couldn't leave--"

THE WITNESS: I tried to --

THE COURT: "-- Grant Park," those words may go out and the jury is directed to disregard them.

BY MR. WEINGLASS:

Q Was there a time when you came upon another person?

A I came upon William Burroughs who had left much earlier than myself who was wandering around in the tear gas with a handkerchief over his face.

Q At the time you met Mr. Burroughs, were you still with Mr. Dellinger?

A No, I had lost Mr. Dellinger.

Q Do you know where Mr. Dellinger went?

A No, I didn't know at the time where he was.

Q After you rejoined Mr. Burroughs, where did you go?

A We continued trying to reach Michigan Avenue. We went to one bridge, soldiers blocking our way and told us we were not to cross the bridge into the city.

Q Where did you go after that?

A I asked them where to go. They said they didn't know. I kept asking and they pointed north. So finally we went way, way north to the very end of the park and found an open bridge.

Q Before coming to the end of the park, did you attempt to cross a second bridge?

A I think I tried to cross three bridges.

Q And did you succeed in getting over any of them.

A No.

Q Why were you unable to get over the bridges?

A There were soldiers in the way.

MR. FORAN: Objection. He testified to that.

THE COURT: I sustain the objection to the question.

BY MR. WEINGLASS:

Q Mr. Ginsberg, I show you a photograph marked D-158 for identification and I ask you if you can identify that photograph.

A Yes.

Q What is that photograph? What does that photograph depict?

A It is a picture of the front line of marchers as I described it before consisting of William Burroughs on the extreme right, Jean Genet, Richard Seaver, his editor at Grove, myself with the flowers that I described, and on my right Michael Cooper who is a British photographer who did the front photograph of the Beatles Sergeant Pepper Album. We were at that point chanting. My mouth is open chanting, and we were marching forward, leading the line of march behind Mr. Dellinger.

Q Was this before the march was stopped?

A Yes.

MR. WEINGLASS: If the Court please, I tender into evidence D-158 for identification as Defendants' Exhibit D-158, the photograph being shown to the Government.

MR. FORAN: No objection.

THE COURT: With no objection, Defendants' Exhibit 158 for identification may be admitted into evidence as Defendants' Exhibit 158.

(The said document, so offered and received in evidence, was marked Defendants' Exhibit 158.)

BY MR. WEINGLASS:

Q Now, Mr. Ginsberg, you have indicated you have known Jerry Rubin since 1965?

A Yes.

Q Would you indicate to the Court and jury whether or not you have ever seen him smoke a cigarette?

A I don't remember.

THE COURT: I didn't hear the answer.
Miss Reporter, will you read the answer.

(Answer read.)

BY MR. WEINGLASS:

Q I mean a tobacco cigarette.

A Offhand, no, I don't remember.

Q Did you ever see Jerry Rubin wearing a helmet during the week of the Convention?

A No.

Q During the week of the convention and the events that you have testified to, did you ever hear either the defendant Jerry Rubin or the defendant Abbie Hoffman encourage or incite people to violent acts?

MR. FORAN: Objection.

THE COURT: I sustain the objection.

BY MR. WEINGLASS:

Q Did you ever hear the defendant Abbie Hoffman during convention week tell people to carry bricks or throw bricks?

A No.

Q Did you ever hear the defendant Abbie Hoffman during convention week tell people to take the Hilton Hotel?

A No.

Q Did you hear the defendant Abbie Hoffman during convention week tell people to fight for the park?

A No.

MR. FORAN: Your Honor, he has never -- it hasn't been established in a single instance that he has been with Abbie Hoffman on any of the occasions that the evidence shows he said those things.

THE COURT: Of course not. Unless the witness was present on every occasion when the defendant Hoffman was present, he isn't qualified to answer. Therefore, I treat the objection as an objection to all of the questions and strike the answers of the witness and direct the jury to disregard them.

BY MR. WEINGLASS:

Q During convention week did you ever hear the defendant Abbie Hoffman address an assemblage of people?

A No.

Q I direct your attention specifically to Tuesday morning --

THE COURT: The answer was no.

MR. WEINGLASS: Pardon me?

THE COURT: The answer was no.

BY MR. WEINGLASS:

Q Directing your attention to Tuesday morning at the sunrise service, did you hear the defendant Abbie Hoffman address the assemblage?

MR. FORAN: I object to that, your Honor.

THE COURT: I sustain the objection. The answer was no.

THE WITNESS: Well, I was present on Tuesday morning when there was a press conference.

MR. WEINGLASS: I am talking about Tuesday morning at your sunrise service.

THE WITNESS: Oh, go ahead.

BY MR. WEINGLASS:

Q Did you hear the defendant address the group at that time?

MR. FORAN: Objection, your Honor, as asked and answered. He said no.

THE COURT: It has been answered. I sustain the objection.

BY MR. WEINGLASS:

Q Now, Mr. Ginsberg, you have had extensive training in Zen and in other religions of the East, have you not?

MR. FORAN: Objection, your Honor.

THE COURT: I sustain the objection.

BY MR. WEINGLASS:

Q Have you acquired an expertise in the area of peaceful intent and peaceful assembly?

MR. FORAN: I object to that, your Honor.

THE COURT: I sustain the objection.

MR. WEINGLASS: Your Honor, the witness was qualified at the beginning of his direct testimony as an expert in the area of chant, peaceful assembly, calming of crowds, and I think he should be permitted to testify in the area of his expertise.

THE COURT: I will let my ruling stand on the objection to the question.

BY MR. WEINGLASS:

Q Did you see during convention week either the defendant Jerry Rubin or the defendant Abbie Hoffman or any of the other defendants who are seated at this table commit an act or make a speech or do anything, do any other thing to violate the precepts of your own philosophy?

MR. FORAN: Objection.

THE COURT: I sustain the objection.

MR. WEINGLASS: I have no further questions.

THE COURT: You may cross-examine.

MR. FORAN: Your Honor, I have to get some materials to properly carry on my cross-examination of this witness. It will take me some time to go downstairs to get them.

THE COURT: How long will it take?

MR. FORAN: I think at least several minutes, your Honor, ten, fifteen minutes.

THE COURT: Are you suggesting we recess?

MR. FORAN: I would think possibly yes, your Honor, because I would just get back up here and get started.

THE COURT: You mean recess until the afternoon?

MR. FORAN: After lunch.

THE COURT: All right. We will go until two o'clock.

MR. WEINGLASS: Your Honor --

MR. KUNSTLER: Your Honor, we have witnesses who are leaving the country this afternoon who are presently here. I don't think there should be any delay in the cross-examination.

MR. FORAN: Your Honor, after each --

MR. WEINGLASS: Wait --

MR. KUNSTLER: Mr. Foran, may I finish my statement?

MR. FORAN: Excuse me, Mr. Kunstler.

MR. KUNSTLER: We have two witnesses in the witness room now waiting around here for two days. One is leaving the country tomorrow morning and must testify or we lose him forever, and the other has to return to the West Coast.

THE COURT: I have granted the request of the defendant --

MR. KUNSTLER: We asked for five minutes two days ago in front of this jury and you refused to give it to us.

MR. FORAN: Your Honor, on every --

THE COURT: You will have to cease that disrespectful tone.

MR. KUNSTLER: That is not disrespect; that is an angry tone, your Honor.

THE COURT: Yes, it is. Yes, it is. I will grant the motion of the Government.

MR. KUNSTLER: You refused us five minutes the other day.

MR. FORAN: Your Honor, on every --

THE COURT: You are going to have to learn --

MR. KUNSTLER: I am trying to learn.

THE COURT: I have given up trying to point it out to you.

MR. KUNSTLER: Why the different treatment?

THE COURT: I will not sit here and have you assume a disrespectful tone to the Court.

MR. KUNSTLER: This is not disrespect.

THE COURT: Yes, it is.

MR. KUNSTLER: I am asking you to explain to the defense which claims it is getting different treatment, why a simple request of five minutes was not granted.

MR. FORAN: Your Honor, may I comment that after the direct examination of every single Government witness in this case the defense had a recess to prepare their cross-examination. That was after 54 witnesses. Every one had a recess.

MR. KUNSTLER: Your Honor, this is the grossest statement I have ever heard in a courtroom. This jury doesn't know that after every Government witness -- we might as well tell them -- there is a series of documents that are given to the defense and the defense must read, and that is the only reason the request was granted. They have no documents --

MR. FORAN: That is right, your Honor. That is --

MR. KUNSTLER: They must go on.

MR. FORAN: We don't -- it is a two-way street -- it is a one-way street.

MR. KUNSTLER: They have no documents to read.

MR. FORAN: Your Honor --

MR. KUNSTLER: It is a one-way street, your Honor. That is what we are on.

MR. FORAN: From the Government to the defense, your Honor.

THE COURT: Now, sir, --

MR. KUNSTLER: We are on a one-way street, your Honor. Five minutes we requested from you.

THE COURT: Mr. Kunstler --

MR. KUNSTLER: Your Honor, what else can I think?

THE COURT: I have admonished you time and again to be respectful to the Court. I have been respectful to you.

MR. KUNSTLER: Your Honor, this is not disrespect for anybody but --

THE COURT: You are shouting at the Court.

MR. KUNSTLER: Oh, your Honor --

THE COURT: Shouting at the Court the way you do --

MR. KUNSTLER: Everyone has shouted from time to time, including your Honor. This is not a situation --

THE COURT: Make a note of that, please. I have never, --

MR. KUNSTLER: Voices have been raised --

THE COURT: I never shouted at you during this trial.

MR. KUNSTLER: Your Honor, your voice has been raised.

THE COURT: You have been disrespectful.

MR. KUNSTLER: It is not disrespectful, your Honor.

THE COURT: And sometimes worse than that.

THE WITNESS: O-o-m-m-m-m.

THE COURT: Will you step off the witness stand, please, and I direct you not to talk with anybody about this case or let anybody speak with you about it until you resume the stand at two o'clock, at which time you are directed to return for further examination.

MR. KUNSTLER: He was trying to calm us both down, your Honor.

THE COURT: Oh, no. I needed no calming down.

MR. KUNSTLER: Your Honor has --

THE COURT: I am pointing out to a lawyer that we will not tolerate disrespect in this court.

MR. KUNSTLER: Your Honor, how --

THE COURT: That will be all.

MR. KUNSTLER: What about our witnesses who have to leave the country? You are depriving us of these witnesses.

THE COURT: We will recess, Mr. Marshal, until two o'clock.

MR. KUNSTLER: Oh, that is unfair.

THE COURT: Ladies and gentlemen of the jury, I almost forgot my orders to you. I am sure you know them. I direct you not to talk with anybody about this case or not to let anybody speak with you about the case. Do not discuss the case among yourselves. I order you not to read the newspapers or any other journals. I order you not to listen to radio or television or look at television. If anybody attempts to communicate with you about this case, please bring it to the attention of the United States Marshal who will in turn lay the matter before me.

Two o'clock.

MR. KUNSTLER: Your Honor, before the court adjourns, can we come back at 1:30? It is an hour and a half --

THE COURT: I am sorry. Two o'clock, sir.

(Whereupon a recess was had at 11:50 o'clock, a.m. until 2:00 o'clock, p.m. of the same day, December 12, 1969.)

IN THE UNITED STATES DISTRICT COURT
NORTHERN DISTRICT OF ILLINOIS
EASTERN DIVISION

UNITED STATES OF AMERICA vs. DAVID T. DELLINGER, et al., Defendants.	))))))	69 CR 180

Before Judge Hoffman and a Jury,
Friday, December 12, 1969,
2:00 o'clock p.m.

Trial resumed pursuant to recess.

Present:

Mr. Foran
Mr. Schultz
Mr. Cubbage

Mr. Kunstler
Mr. Weinglass

THE CLERK: No. 69 CR 180. United States of America vs. David T. Dellinger, et al. Cause on trial.

(The following proceedings were had in open court, in the presence and hearing of the jury:)

THE COURT: Is the witness here?

ALLEN GINSBERG,

heretofore called as a witness on behalf of the defendants, and having been heretofore first duly sworn, resumed the stand and testified further as follows:

THE COURT: As I understand it, you had finished your direct?

MR. WEINGLASS: Yes.

THE COURT: You may cross-examine.

MR. FORAN: Mr. Ginsberg, calling your attention to --
Excuse me.
I think that the government would like to withdraw its objection to Defendants' Exhibits 152 and 153.

THE COURT: D-152. Was that a journal, a daily journal?

MR. FORAN: Yes, one was a poem in his daily journal, your Honor, and I think the other one was a poem that was published in a press release or something.

MR. WEINGLASS: Not a poem; it is a very brief message.

THE COURT: Defendants' Exhibit 153 was written by the witness, as I understand it, and my note says it was printed in some newspaper. 152 was offered, was it?

MR. FORAN: Yes, your Honor. It was in a journal. It was one page of a journal, I believe.

THE COURT: Objection was sustained. You now wish to withdraw that objection?

MR. FORAN: Yes, your Honor, I do.

THE COURT: You may withdraw the objection and with no objection, Defendants' Exhibit 152 for identification will be admitted into evidence as Defendants' Exhibit 152.

(Said document, so offered and received in evidence, was marked Defendants' Exhibit 152.)

THE COURT: The other one was what, 153?

MR. FORAN: 153.

THE COURT: Objection to that was sustained and you wish to withdraw the objection?

MR. FORAN: Yes, your Honor.

THE COURT: You may withdraw the objection to Defendants' Exhibit 153 and with no objection, Defendants' Exhibit 153 for identification will be admitted into evidence as Defendants' Exhibit 153.

(Said document, so offered and received in evidence, was marked Defendants' Exhibit 153.)

THE COURT: Having done that, I must accord the defense lawyers a chance to examine the witness about those exhibits.

MR. FORAN: I think that would be fair, your Honor, yes.

THE COURT: You may, if you like, examine the witness in respect to those two exhibits, sir.

DIRECT EXAMINATION
(Resumed:)

BY MR. WEINGLASS:

Q Mr. Ginsberg, with respect to D-152 which is now in evidence, can you once again relate to the court and jury what that is?

A Is that the newspaper clipping from "Rat"?

Q No, I am sorry. Maybe I had better -- I am sure you are not familiar with the numbers.

A No.

Q D-152 is a poem.

A Oh, yes. It is notations I made in my journal about the Chicago Convention on flying to Chicago on that Saturday preceding the convention, August 24th. It is what I was writing down from my head and heart, what I felt about what was going to happen and what I felt about it, so I tried to articulate where everybody was and where I was in it, what the Yippie convention was going to be like.

Q Could you now read to the jury that poem?

A Gladly. I believe you have the text.

August 24, 1968

"Going to Chicago"

"22,000 feet over Hazed square Vegetable planet Floor
Approaching Chicago to Die or flying over Earth another
    40 years
to die--Indifferent, and afraid, that the bone-shattering
    bullet
be the same as the vast evaporation-of-phenomena Cancer
Come true in an old man's bed. Or Historic
Fire-Heaven Descending 22,000 years End th' Atomic
    Aeon

The Lake's blue again, Sky's the same baby, tho' papers &
    Noses
rumor tar spread through the Natural Universe'll make
    Angel's feet sticky.
I heard the Angel King's voice, a bodiless tuneful teenager
Eternal in my own heart saying "Trust the Purest Joy -
Democratic Anger is an Illusion, Democratic Joy is God
Our Father is baby blue, the original face you see Sees
    You-"

How, thru Conventional Police & Revolutionary Fury
Remember the Helpless order the Police Armed to protect,
The Helpless Freedom the Revolutionary Conspired to
    honor-
I am the Angel King sang the Angel King
as mobs in Amphitheaters, Streets, Colosseums Parks and
    offices
Scream in despair over Meat and Metal Microphone"

Q I now show you what is marked D-153 for identification, which is a publication of yours that appeared in "Rat", I believe you testified, three days before the convention began?

A Yes.

Q Could you read that to the jury?

A "Magic Password Bulletin. Physic Jujitsu.

"In case of hysteria, solitary or communal, the magic password is Om, same as Aum, which cuts through all emergency illusions. Pronounce Om from the middle of the body, diaphragm or solar plexus. Ten people humming Om can calm down one hundred. One hundred people humming Om can regulate the metabolism of a thousand. A thousand bodies vibrating Om can immobilize an entire downtown Chicago street full of scared humans, uniformed or naked.

Signed, Allen Ginsberg, Ed Sanders.

"Om will be practiced on the beach at sunrise ceremonies with Allen and Ed."

Q Now, Mr. Ginsberg, where you say a thousand people chanting Om could immobilize an area in downtown Chicago, what did you mean by that?

MR. FORAN: Objection.

THE COURT: The words are there, whatever they mean.

MR. WEINGLASS: He will not be permitted the courtesy of explaining the words he used?

THE COURT: I will always be courteous to a witness, Mr. Weinglass.

MR. WEINGLASS: Will you permit this witness to --

THE COURT: I have accorded this witness every courtesy but we don't permit him to do what the law doesn't permit me to let him do.

MR. WEINGLASS: And I understand the law does not permit this witness to explain his own poetry?

THE COURT: The words are clear. They are simple words. The jury heard them. Let the jury conclude what they mean.

MR. WEINGLASS: And they must do that without the assistance of the author telling them what he meant when he wrote them?

MR. FORAN: Your Honor, if Mr. Ginsberg can give some short explanation of it, I have no objection.

THE COURT: You want it --

MR. FORAN: I have no objection.

THE COURT: If there is no objection, I will let him do it. I don't concede his right to do it but with no objection, I will permit him to.
What is your question?

BY MR. WEINGLASS:

Q Could you explain to the Court and jury what you meant in that last statement of your message?

A Immobilize an entire downtown Chicago street full of scared human beings, uniformed or naked -- by immobilize I meant shut down the mental machinery which repeats over and over again the images of fear which are scaring people in uniform, that is to say, the police officers, or the demonstrators whom I refer to as naked, meaning naked emotionally and perhaps, hopefully, naked physically.

Q And what did you intend to create by having that mechanism shut down?

A A completely peaceful realization of the fact that we were all stuck in the same street, place, terrified of each other, and reacting in panic and hysteria rather than reacting with awareness of each other as human beings, as people with bodies that actually feel, can chant and pray and have a certain sense of vibration to each other or tenderness to each other which is what basically everybody wants rather than fear.

MR. WEINGLASS: I have nothing further.

THE COURT: Cross-examination.

CROSS-EXAMINATION

BY MR. FORAN:

Q Mr. Ginsberg, calling your attention to Monday night, August 26, 1968, I think you testified that you were in Lincoln Park near the barricade?

A Yes.

Q Where was that barricade, do you recall?

A I think down in the center of the park. It was dark and I don't know its location in the park. It was deep into the park, I think on the right if you enter from the Lincoln Hotel.

Q How long was it?

A At the edge of a field --

Q How long was it, Mr. Ginsberg?

A Not very long. It was about -- the barricade part with the tin cans, about 20 feet wide.

Q Just about 20 feet?

A Yes, as I remember it.

Q Would you indicate here in the courtroom how far 20 feet is?

A The length of the wooden rail in front of the jury box.

Q The jury rail, about as long as the jury rail?

A That part that I was in front of. I think it was circular, extended around, but I didn't see that part of it. It was dark and there were many people.

Q Did you only see a part about as long as the jury box?

A Yes, because I was standing right next to it.

Q How high was it?

A It moved around at one point -- that is, it changed at one point. One of the kids put a table or put a trash can, I think, up on top of a table, and then took it down.

Q Was that the highest part?

A Yes. There were people standing on the table part that I saw.

Q What was the barricade made of?

A What I saw was just materials that were around there, trash cans, and -- I wasn't sure. It was dark. I think there was wooden fencing or wooden horses.

Q Was there anybody at the barricade who had a bullhorn?

A No, I didn't see anyone with a bullhorn.

Q Did you see anybody there who had any flags?

A No.

Q Did you hear any shouting at the barricade?

A Yes. That's why I went to it, there was unpleasant shouting, provocative noise, and a bit of drunken noise there. That is why I went over there and started chanting.

Q Do you remember what they were? Was some of the noise chants other than the chants you were leading, Mr. Ginsberg?

A Yes. That is why I went there, to transform the chanting.

Q Do you remember any of those chants?

A I heard "Pig" shouted.

Q Did you hear "Hell, no, we won't go"?

A No, I don't remember specifically what I did hear. The thing that disturbed me most was the banging, the metallic banging on the -- the drum-like banging, a war cry drum-like banging on the waste barrels.

Q How many people were there?

A A hundred, two hundred, right directly around the barricade.

Q Was that all you could see within your range of vision?

A That's all I could see right immediately around the barricade. There were a lot of people around the park looking down on it, too.

Q How many would you say altogether?

A There were thousands more. I didn't go through the whole park. I just went to this area.

Q Were there any police?

A Yes, very far away down at the other end of the field of the barricade.

Q How were they standing?

A I couldn't see because they were like a hundred -- what seemed to me like the length of a football-like field or athletic field away.

Q Were they lined up casually or in a kind of military-like formation?

A I didn't see the police. I saw police lights.

Q Did you see a police car come from the direction of the police line right toward the barricade that had a loudspeaker on its roof?

A No. I saw a police car come from the opposite direction behind us, behind the barricade, rather than from where I thought the police were.

Q But you didn't see any police car come from the direction of the police lines toward the barricade?

A No.

Q Did you hear anything over a loud-speaker announcing that the park was closed and anyone remaining in the park should be arrested?

A No, I didn't hear -- I don't remember hearing it.

Q Did you see anyone throwing any rocks at the police?

A At the police lines?

Q Yes.

A No. The police lines were much too far away. I didn't see anybody throw any rocks. I saw people banging and making noise.

Q Did you see anyone throwing any tiles, flat roof tiles?

A No.

Q Did you see anyone throwing any bottles?

A No. As I say, the police were, it looked like, a quarter of a mile away.

Q Did the police -- were you there when the police came forward?

A No. I started moving away when the police car crashed down into the crowd.

Q Now what was the first thing you heard of that police car? You were there and you were chanting Om, as I recall.

A Om.

Q And then something distracted that chant?

A Yes, the movement of the car.

Q Did you hear some breaking glass?

A Yes, quite a bit of breaking glass.

Q Was the broken glass in the police car?

A Well, it sounded as if the car were riding over glass or bottles. As soon as the car started --

Q How far away were you from the car, by the way?

A About 35 feet.

Q Did you see the car?

A Yes, I saw it moving into the crowd.

Q Did you see if it had all of its windows broken?

A When I first saw the car, no.

Q Did you see all of the windows in it broken?

A No, I didn't actually. I heard the crash of glass, though.

Q Did you hear anyone shouting, "Kill the pigs. Get them. Get them!"?

A No. I heard people saying, "Get out. The police are coming."

Q Did you hear anybody say, "Get those pigs in the car"?

A No. I might explain I continued chanting.

Q Where did the car go?

A It went down in through the crowd and into the barricade. People moved away because it was moving slower as it got into the middle. There was a crashing of glass. I started moving away. I started turning and going because it seemed to me that --

Q Where did you go then, Mr. Ginsberg?

A I continued chanting and started walking out of the park.

Q Were you there --
By the way, did you see the tear gas go off?

A After I started moving away, there was tear gas that I smelled, yes.

Q Did you see it or did you just smell it?

A I saw it also, yes.

Q Where did it go off with respect to the barricade?

A It looked to me like a wall of tear gas in the middle of the empty space playing field, I thought, and then more coming, falling down in the park behind the barricade where we were.

Q Where was the tear gas with respect to the barricade?

A At first I thought it was -- at the beginning as I was looking back, because I was already walking away when the car came on the other side of the barricade toward the police, but then when I was walking out, it was right in the middle of the whole park. I don't know where it was coming from actually.

BY MR. FORAN:

Q Now, on the 28th, you eventually got into that line of march on Columbus Drive near the bandshell, didn't you?

A That is on Wednesday?

MR. WEINGLASS: Will the prosecutor indicate the date by the day of the week.

THE WITNESS: Wednesday.

MR. FORAN: Wednesday.

BY THE WITNESS:

A I got actually very early into the line.

BY MR. FORAN:

Q You were close up front, weren't you?

A Yes.

Q Near Mr. Dellinger?

A Yes, when the marches started moving, I was about 20, 15 feet behind him.

Q Was Mr. Dellinger on the bullhorn?

A Yes.

Q Were there others using the same bullhorn, or were there other bullhorns there, do you recall?

A I think in the march, at the head of the march, there was only one bullhorn that I saw.

Q You saw only one?

A Yes. I think there were bullhorns out among the police, though.

Q I mean among the marchers.

A At the head of the marchers, just the one bullhorn. There was a kid carrying it before Mr. Dellinger or behind Mr. Dellinger.

Q Now, when did you start this kind of special study of chanting, Mr. Ginsberg?

A I met a Swami Shivananda in 1962 in Rishikesh, R-i-s-h-i-k-e-s-h, India, which is where the Ganges comes out of the Himalayan Mountains and into the Gangetic Plain at an Ashram of Shivananda, and he had the mantra, the Hare Krishna mantra, printed in a book and he pointed my attention to it.

Q Was your attention called to that originally because of your interest in poetry, or because of desire for spiritual uplifting, could you say?

A Swami Shivananda was a poet also, and I told him I was a poet, and he gave me a book called the "Raja Yoga For Americans." He pronounced the word "Om" as part of his ritual.

Q In the discipline, there is a similarity of beauty of sound in poetry and in chanting?

A Yes. In the poem, "Bhagavad-Gita," you know, which is "The Song of God," which is the Bible in India, has as its main character Krishna, who is the person talked about in the Mantra, Hare Krishna.

Q So in a way, some of the chants are poems in themselves.

A Yes, they are identical. Chanting and religious scripture in India, as it is in the West, is identical. Like, our Bible is written in Hebrew poetry, too.

Q And that combination of chanting and poetry has as its purpose a sort of a spiritual uplifting of the audience?

A Physically, really to locate and center you in your body and regulate your breathing, calm your metabolism, and become aware of what is around you.

Q I meant more than just the chanting, itself. I meant the kind of combination of the poetry and the chanting, the recitation of the poetry and the beauty of the sound, itself.

A The recitation of poetry has a secret purpose of regulating your breathing, therefore, regulating the body chemistry, regulating the metabolism, and calming the breathing, actually to calm the breathing, and make it steady and even. Simultaneously the poetry, like the Hare Krishna mantra, suggests images of the blue bodied God Krishna, Preserver of the world.

Q Well, now, on that Exhibit D-151, that is that letterhead --

A YIP Om?

Q No, that was the letterhead of the Yippie organization with the list of names on the side. That is what I referred to as D-151.

MR. FORAN: Could we have it?

MR. KUNSTLER: Yes.

BY MR. FORAN:

Q It is this.

A Yes.

Q You were named as kind of the Yippie religious leader on that letterhead. Do you think in whatever sense you would like to put it that is a fair designation of your connection with the Yippie organization?

A No, because the word leader was one we really tried to get away from, to get away from that authoritarian thing. It was more like --

Q Religious teacher?

A -- religious experimenter, or someone who was interested in experimenting with that, and moving things in that direction.

Q In the context of the Yippie organization?

A Yes, and also in the context of our whole political life, too.

Q And among the others named are Timothy Leary.

A Yes.

Q And Timothy Leary has kind of a religious concept that he attempts to articulate also, doesn't he?

A Yes, it is a religious concept that has a very ancient tradition in Shivite worship and in American Indian worship services or ceremonies.

Q And one of the parts of that religious concept is the religious experience in the use of hallucinogenic drugs, isn't it, Mr. Ginsberg?

A In India, in the Shivite Sect, they refer to it as ganja or bhang, which in Latin is cannabis, and which in the American language is marijuana, or pot or grass.

Q That is one of Mr. Leary's particular propositions of his religious experience, is it not?

A Yes, it is one that he practices, I believe, as an initiate, or member of the Shivite Order which traditionally makes use of that substance as a sacrament.

Q In the course of his teaching, he makes use of those drugs, himself?

A I think he says that they are part of legitimate religious meditation and worship exercises.

Q Now, in the course of your work, itself, Mr. Ginsberg, you go around to various places and recite your poetry?

A Yes.

Q And chant?

A Yes.

Q You chant many times in conjunction with it?

A Yes, as I have done here.

Q Doing both of them at the same time?

A Generally.

Q Generally, for the same purpose, are they in combination?

A Yes, I try to begin by invoking some deeper spirit than intellectual language. I begin really to try to calm my own body, calm myself by chanting, and to calm the audience a little so that they're aware that I am here, that they are sitting there in their bodies, and that we are together in the same room and sharing our feelings.

Q So when you, like in Lincoln Park that Sunday afternoon, when you chanted, and when you recited some of William Blake's poetry, that combination of chanting and poetry, was within the context, as you see it, Mr. Ginsberg, of generating a spiritual and physical uplift to the audience?

A Not so much an uplift, but a calm, a feeling of ease and relaxation to eliminate tension, to eliminate anxiety, to eliminate hysteria, to eliminate the hallucination of scary images of police with --

Q Within that concept of yours as you designate yourself as the religious experimenter of the Yippie Organization, and I don't mean to be tricky at all about this, I mean just to use words that are perhaps --

A Yes.

Q -- familiar, this concept of physical calmness and acceptance is a part of the religious experience that you were attempting to experiment with and teach?

A Yes.

Q Is that a fair statement?

A Yes.

Q And both your poetry and chanting are a part of that same religious experimentation concept?

A Using the term we have on the letterhead there, religion, yes.

Q Religion.

A Yes.

Q Now when you went out to the Coliseum and you met Abbie Hoffman, you said when you met him you kissed him?

A Yes.

Q Is he an intimate friend of yours?

A I felt very intimate with him. I saw he was struggling to manifest a beautiful thing, and I felt very good towards him.

Q And you do consider him an intimate friend of yours?

A I don't see him that often, but I see him often enough and have worked with him often enough to feel intimate with him, yes.

Q You feel pretty much an intimate friend of Jerry Rubin's also?

A Yes, over the years.

Q By the way --

A I have learned from them both.

Q By the way, you were asked on direct examination whether you had seen Jerry Rubin smoke any tobacco.

A Yes.

Q You said no.

A I said I didn't remember seeing him smoke,

Q Have you seen him smoke anything?

A No, I don't remember seeing him smoke anything.

Q When you were asked on direct examination whether you had ever seen him smoke, there was some hesitation until the question was rephrased.

A Yes.

Q Rephrased to tobacco.

A I smoked myself until last year, and I quit smoking, and I don't remember seeing Jerry smoking. I don't know whether he smokes or not, actually. And I was trying to figure out did I remember seeing him smoke or not. That is why I said I didn't remember instead of saying no.

Q So you don't know whether you ever saw him smoke or not?

A I don't remember ever seeing him smoke.

Q Anything?

A Yes.

Q You mean you don't remember?

A I don't remember ever seeing him smoke anything.

Q Meaning you don't remember seeing him smoke anything.
Now, you testified concerning a number of books of poetry that you have written?

A Yes.

Q One of them was the "Empty Mirror."

A Yes, a book of early poems written in 1946 to 1951.

Q You also talked about "In Society."

A Yes.

Q And that is another poem you wrote?

A Yes, it is the transcription of a dream that I had, a night dream.

Q What about "Reality Sandwiches"? That is another book?

A It is a book of poems written over a period from 1953 to 1960. They are all writings like the writing in my journal here.

Q Like the one in your little journal?

A Anything that I wrote down spontaneously at different times registering my feeling, I put down what I had in my mind.

Q In the "Empty Mirror," there is a poem called, "The Night-Apple"?

A Yes.

Q Would you recite that for the jury?

A I would have to have the text to recite it. It is a very short poem. If you will give me the text, I will be glad to.

MR. FORAN: I will mark this Government's Exhibit No. --

MR. CUBBAGE: 59.

MR. FORAN: -- 59 for identification.

(Said exhibit was thereupon marked Government's Exhibit 59 for identification.)

MR. WEINGLASS: If the Court please, I don't want to stand on a technicality, and I don't want to prevent the witness from reading from this poem.

However, there has been a rule that unless an exhibit is in evidence, the witness cannot read from it, and I don't believe the government can introduce an exhibit during our case.

I would be willing to put the exhibit in as our exhibit in order to facilitate the government's cross-examination of this witness.

MR. FORAN: Your Honor, I will be able to handle it, I think.

THE COURT: What is that number of identification?

MR. FORAN: It is Government's Exhibit No. 59 for identification.

BY MR. FORAN:

Q Mr. Ginsberg, I show you Government's Exhibit No. 59 for identification --

A Yes.

Q I call your attention to page 32 of that exhibit. Does that have on page 32 the poem, "The Night-Apple"?

A Yes.

Q When you look at that page, Mr. Ginsberg, does it refresh your recollection of the poem, itself?

A Yes. I wrote it in 1950. That was nineteen years ago. It still looks good.

Q After refreshing your recollection, Mr. Ginsberg, could you recite that poem to the jury?

A Yes. "The Night-Apple."

"Last night I dreamed
of one I loved
for seven long years,
but I saw no face,
only the familiar
presence of the body:
sweat skin eyes
feces urine sperm
saliva all one
odor and mortal taste."

Q Could you explain to the jury what the religious significance of that poem is?

A If you would take a wet dream as a religious experience, I could. It is a description of a wet dream, sir.

Q Now, I call your attention in that same Government's Exhibit No. 59, to page 14.

A Yes.

Q That has on it the poem, "In Society"?

A Right.

Q And is that one of the poems you have written, Mr. Ginsberg?

A Yes, it says on the bottom 1947, it was a dream.

Q Does that refresh your recollection of that poem?

A Yes.

Q After refreshing your recollection, can you recite that poem to the jury?

A Yes, I will read it.

"In Society"

"I walked into the cocktail party
room and found three or four queers
talking together in queertalk.
I tried to be friendly but heard
myself talking to one in hiptalk.
"I'm glad to see you," he said, and
looked away. "Hmn," I mused. The room
was small and had a double-decker
bed in it, and cooking apparatus:
icebox, cabinet, toasters, stove;
the hosts seemed to live with room
enough only for cooking and sleeping.
My remark on this score was under-
stood but not appreciated. I was
offered refreshments, which I accepted.
I ate a sandwich of pure meat; an
enormous sandwich of human flesh,
I noticed, while I was chewing on it,
it also included a dirty asshole.

More company came, including a
fluffy female who looked like
a princess. She glared at me and
said immediately: "I don't like you."
turned her head away, and refused
to be introduced. I said, "What!"
in outrage. "Why you shit-faced fool!"
This got everybody's attention.
"Why you naricissistic bitch! How
can you decide when you don't even
know me," I continued in a violent
and messianic voice, inspired at

last, dominating the whole room."

Dream 1947

It is a record, a literal record of a dream as the other was a literal record of a dream.

Q Can you explain the religious significance of that poetry?

A Actually, yes.

Q Would you explain it to the jury?

A Yes, one of the major yogas, or yoking -- yoga means yoke -- is bringing together the conscious mind with the unconscious mind and is an examination of dream states in an attempt to recollect dream states no matter how difficult they are, no matter how repulsive they are, even if they include hysteria, sandwiches of human flesh, which include dirty assholes, because those are universal images that come in everybody's dreams.

The attempt in yoga is to enlarge consciousness, to be conscious that one's own consciousness will include everything which occurs within the body and the mind.

As part of the practice of poetry, I have always kept records of dreams whenever I have remembered them and have tried not to censor them so that I would have all the evidence to examine in light of day so that I would find out who I was unconsciously.

Part of Zen meditation and part of yoga meditation consists in the objective impersonal examination of the rise and the fall and disappearance of thoughts in the mind. All thoughts, whether they be thoughts of sleeping with one's mother, which is universal, or sleeping with one's father, which is also universal thought, or becoming an angel, or flying, or attending a cocktail party and being afraid of being put down, and then getting hysterical. In other words, the attempt is to reclaim the unconscious, to write down in the light of day what is going on in the deepest meditation of night and dream state so it is part of a yoga which involves bridging the difference between public, as in this courtroom, and private subjective: Public, which is conscious, which we can say to others in family situations, and private which is what we know and tell only our deepest friends.

Q Thank you.

MR. FORAN: Your Honor, I have marked another one Government's Exhibit No. 60 for identification.

(The said document was thereupon marked Government's Exhibit No. 60 for identification.)

BY MR. FORAN:

Q You also wrote a book of poems called "Reality Sandwiches," didn't you?

A Yes.

Q In there, there is a poem called, "Love Poem on Theme by Whitman"?

A Yes.

Q I show you Government's Exhibit No. 60 for identification, and I call your attention to page 41, and I ask you whether or not that refreshes your recollection of that poem?

A Yes.

Q After having refreshed your recollection, would you recite that to the jury?

A "Love Poem on Theme by Whitman," Walt Whitman being our celebrated bard, national prophet. The poem begins with a quotation of a line by Walt Whitman---it begins with Walt Whitman's line:

"I'll go into the bedroom silently and lie down between the
bridegroom and the bride,
those bodies fallen from heaven stretched out waiting naked and
restless,
arms resting over their eyes in the darkness,
bury my face in their shoulders and breasts, breathing their skin,
and stroke and kiss neck and mouth and make back be open
and known,
legs raised up crook'd to receive, cock in the darkness driven
tormented and attacking
roused up from hole to itching head,
bodies locked shuddering naked, hot lips and buttocks screwed
into each other
and eyes, eyes glinting and charming, widening into looks and
abandon,
and moans of movement, voices, hands in air, hands between
thighs,
hands in moisture on softened hips, throbbing contraction of
bellies
till the white come flow in the swirling sheets,
and the bride cry for forgiveness, and the groom be covered with
tears of passion and compassion,
and I rise up from the bed replenished with last intimate gestures
and kisses of farewell -
all before the mind wakes, behind shades and closed doors in
darkened house
where the inhabitants roam unsatisfied in the night,
nude ghosts seeking each other out in the silence."

Q Would you explain the religious significance of that poem?

A As part of our nature, as part of our human nature we have many loves, many of which are suppressed, many of which are denied, many of which we deny to ourselves. He said that the reclaiming of those loves and the becoming aware of those loves was the only way that this nation could save itself and become a democratic and spiritual republic.

He said that unless there were an infusion of feeling, of tenderness, of fearlessness, of spirituality, of natural sexuality, of natural delight in each other's bodies into the hardened materialistic, cynical, life denying, clearly competitive, afraid, scared, armored bodies, there would be no chance for spiritual democracy to take root in America and he defined that tenderness between the citizens as, in his words, an Adhesiveness, a natural tenderness flowing between all citizens, not only men and women but also a tenderness between men and men, as part of our democratic heritage, part of the adhesiveness which would make the democracy function; that men could work together not as competitive beasts but as tender lovers and fellows.

So he projected, from his own desire and from his own unconscious, a sexual urge which he felt was normal to the unconscious of most people, though forbidden for the most part to take part.

"I will go into the bedroom silently and lie down between the bridegroom and the bride."

He projected as he did in another poem, Orgy, "City of Orgies", as he called New York, he projected physical affection even to the sexual -- or his phrase is "physical affection and all that is latently implied" between citizen and citizen as part of the adhesiveness which would make us function together as a community rather than as a nation "among the fabled damned of nations", which was his phrase in the essay "Democratic Vistas."

Walt Whitman is one of my spiritual teachers and I am following him in this poem, taking off from a line of his own and projecting my own actual unconscious feelings, of which I don't have shame, sir, which I feel are basically charming actually.

THE COURT: I didn't hear that last word.

THE WITNESS: Charming.

Q When you were out at Columbus and Balbo when Mr. Dellinger was on the bullhorn, did you hear Mr. Dellinger say over the bullhorn, "I want to make it clear that there is a core group and we hope it is as large a group as possible who is going to stay here for now and at some point we may start, and we are staying here, and if we move at some point forward, of course the road is blocked -- if we move at some point forward, we will do it as we move."
Did you hear Mr. Dellinger say that over a bullhorn?

A I don't remember the exact words but I remember similar words. I don't remember, "Do it as we move." I don't quite understand that, but, yes.

Q Do you remember him saying there is plenty of chance for those who wish to engage in the mobile tactics to go and do them, and I am sure that we will do mobile tactics tonight? Do you remember him saying that?

A Yes, but I remember him saying that -- asking those who wanted to do mobile tactics to go away because it was to be a peaceful march and he wanted the core group to stay there for a peaceful march. I think I mentioned that before in my testimony. He reiterated that several times, was very clear about it.

Q Do you remember him saying, "I can't tell you every detail of what is going to happen, but whatever happens, it is going to help us"? Do you remember him saying that?

A No.

Q Did you hear anyone on that bullhorn at the intersection of Columbus and Balbo say, "Break up into small groups and go into the Loop and get into the hotels and the stores and the theatres"? Did you hear anybody say that?

A No. I heard, there was a point when someone announced that all those who wished to stay and continue the march and risk arrest should stay seated, I believe; those who wanted to proffer or offer passive resistance, who wanted to insist on their rights to march, should stay and sit down. Those who wanted to leave should get up and move out now before the arrests began.

Q Do you remember when you were standing there with Mr. Dellinger at Columbus and Balbo Drive you said there were some marshals right there, weren't there?

A In front of --

Q Right in front, right between you and Mr. Dellinger?

A Well, we were walking -- yes. At other times I was with Mr. Dellinger side by side when he was consulting with the police officers.

Q Did you hear any marshals come up to Mr. Dellinger and say, "We are through the police lines. We are in Michigan Avenue. The street is ours"?

A No; definitely not, in fact.

MR. FORAN: I have no further questions.

THE COURT: Redirect examination.

THE WITNESS: I wonder if --

REDIRECT EXAMINATION

BY MR. WEINGLASS:

Q Mr. Ginsberg, could you indicate to the Court and jury when Walt Whitman wrote the poetry?

A He wrote his poetry up to and around the time of the Civil War and past. The particular poem that I am talking about is probably after the Civil War.
The poem I read, by the way, I would like to date the poem that I read.

THE COURT: All the lawyer asked was something about the late Walt Whitman, nothing else, sir.

THE WITNESS: Yes.

BY MR. WEINGLASS:

Q Could you indicate to the Court and jury what place in American history this man had?

MR. FORAN: I object to that, your Honor. We didn't have any of Walt Whitman's poetry read here.

THE COURT: I sustain the objection.

THE WITNESS: Oh, we had one line read, sir. We had the key line.

THE COURT: I am not going to go into --

THE WITNESS: Excuse me. I am sorry.

THE COURT: I am not going to go into Walt Whitman's reputation in literary history. I don't believe that is a part of this redirect examination.

BY MR. WEINGLASS:

Q Do you have a poem before you entitled "Howl"?

A No, I don't have that. It is in another book than this one.

Q Can you recall that poem without reference to the other book?

A I can't recite it all. I know fragments of it, yes.

Q Could you recite to the Court and jury the fragments that you can recall?

A "I saw the best minds of my generation destroyed by madness,
starving, hysterical naked,
dragging themselves through the Negro streets at dawn looking for
an angry fix,
angelheaded hipsters searching for the ancient heavenly connection
to the starry dynamo in the machinery of night,
who poverty and tatters and hollow-eyed and high sat up smoking
in the supernatural darkness of cold-water flats floating
across the tops of cities contemplating jazz,
who bared their brains to Heaven under the El and saw Mohammedan
angels staggering on tenement roofs illuminated,
who crossed through the United States, crosscountry in 72 hours
to find out if I had a vision or you had a vision or he had
a vision, to find out Eternity,
who were expelled from the academies for crazy, for publishing
obscene odes on the windows of the skull,
who broke down crying in white gymnasiums naked and trembling
before the machinery of other skeletons,
who were dragged off the roof waving genitals and manuscripts,
who screamed in delight in police cars for committing no crime
but their own wild cooking, pederasty and intoxication,
who lit cigarettes in boxcars, boxcars, boxcars, racketing through
snow toward lonesome farms in grandfather night,
who moved through universities with radiant cool eyes among the
scholars of war, hallucinating Arkansas and Blake-light
tragedy,
who coughed on the sixth floor of Harlem surrounded with
orange crates of theology,
who protested the narcotic tobacco haze of capitalism,
who chained themselves to subways for the endless ride from Battery
to holy Bronx on benzedrine until the noise of wheels and
children brought them down shuddering, battered bleak of
brain all drained of brilliance in the drear light of Zoo,
....
What sphinx of cement and aluminum bashed open these skulls and
ate up their brains and imagination?
Moloch! Solitude! Filth! Ugliness! Ashcans and unobtainable
dollars! Boys sobbing in armies, children weeping under
the stairways, old men weeping in the park!
Moloch! Moloch! Nightmare of Moloch! Moloch the loveless,
Moloch the heavy judger of men!
Moloch the crossbone soulless jailhouse and congress of sorrows!
Moloch whose buildings are judgment! Moloch the vast stone
of war! Moloch the stunned government!

Moloch whose ear is a smoking tomb! Moloch whose blood is running money! Moloch whose soul is electricity and banks! Moloch whose smokestacks and antennae crown the cities. Moloch whose fate is a cloud of sexless hydrogen! Moloch whose name is the Mind!

Moloch in whom I sit lonely! Moloch in whom I am a consciousness without a body! Moloch that entered my soul early! Moloch whom I abandon! Wake up in Moloch! Light streaming out of the sky!

Moloch! Moloch! Robot apartments, invisible suburbs, skeleton treasuries, demonic industries, monstrous bombs!

They broke their backs lifting Moloch to Heaven! Pavement, trees, radios, tons, lifting the city to Heaven which exists and is everywhere about us!

Dreams, adorations, religions, illuminations! Ten years animal screams and suicides!

Real holy laughter in the river! They saw it all! The wild eyes, the holy yells! They jumped off the roof to suicide waving, carrying flowers, down to the river, into the street!"

That is fragmentary.

MR. WEINGLASS: I have nothing further.

THE COURT: Within the limits of that examination, I will permit further examination.

MR. FORAN: No, thanks.

THE COURT: Nothing? You may go, sir.

THE WITNESS: Thank you.

(Witness excused.)

THE COURT: Call your next witness.

CITY LIGHTS PUBLICATIONS

Antonin Artaud, ANTHOLOGY $3.00
Julian Beck, THE LIFE OF THE THEATRE $3.50
Robert Bly, THE TEETH-MOTHER NAKED AT LAST $1.00
Michael Bowen, JOURNEY TO NEPAL $2.50
Paul Bowles, A HUNDRED CAMELS IN THE COURTYARD $1.25
Charles Bukowski, ERECTIONS, EJACULATIONS, EXHIBITIONS AND GENERAL TALES OF ORDINARY MADNESS $4.50
Charles Bukowski, NOTES OF A DIRTY OLD MAN $3.00
William S. Burroughs & Allen Ginsberg, THE YAGE LETTERS $1.50
Neal Cassady, THE FIRST THIRD $3.00
CITY LIGHTS JOURNAL No. 3 $2.50
Gregory Corso, GASOLINE $1.00
Albert Cossery, MEN GOD FORGOT $1.50
René Daumal, MOUNT ANALOGUE $2.00
Alexandra David-Neel, SECRET ORAL TEACHINGS IN TIBETAN BUDDHIST SECTS $2.00
Diane diPrima, REVOLUTIONARY LETTERS $2.50
George Dowden, BIBLIOGRAPHY OF ALLEN GINSBERG $17.50 (cloth)
Paul Erlich, ECO-CATASTROPHE 50¢
Ernest Fenollosa, THE CHINESE WRITTEN CHARACTER AS A MEDIUM FOR POETRY $1.50
Lawrence Ferlinghetti, CITY LIGHTS ANTHOLOGY $5.00
Lawrence Ferlinghetti, PICTURES OF THE GONE WORLD $1.00
Jean Genet, MAY DAY SPEECH $1.00
Allen Ginsberg, THE FALL OF AMERICA $3.00
Allen Ginsberg, HOWL AND OTHER POEMS $1.50
Allen Ginsberg, INDIAN JOURNALS $3.00
Allen Ginsberg, IRON HORSE $3.00
Allen Ginsberg, KADDISH AND OTHER POEMS $1.50
Allen Ginsberg, PLANET NEWS $2.50
Allen Ginsberg, REALITY SANDWICHES $1.50
Ernest Hemingway, COLLECTED POEMS 50¢
Journal for the Protection of All Beings No. 2, ON THE BARRICADES $1.50
Journal for the Protection of All Beings No. 1, GREEN FLAG $1.50
James Joyce, POMES PENYEACH 50¢
Bob Kaufman, GOLDEN SARDINE $1.50
Jack Kerouac, BOOK OF DREAMS $2.50
Jack Kerouac, SCATTERED POEMS $2.00
Philip Lamantia, SELECTED POEMS $1.50
Timothy Leary, EAGLE BRIEF 50¢
Malcolm Lowry, SELECTED POEMS $1.50
Norman Mailer, THE WHITE NEGRO $1.00
Michael McClure, MEAT SCIENCE ESSAYS $2.00
Henri Michaux, MISERABLE MIRACLE $2.00
Daniel Moore, BURNT HEART $2.50
Mohammed Mrabet, M'HASHISH $1.50
Harold Norse, HOTEL NIRVANA $2.00
Frank O'Hara, LUNCH POEMS $1.25
Charles Olson, CALL ME ISHMAEL $2.00
Thomas Parkinson, PROTECT THE EARTH $1.50
Kenneth Patchen, LOVE POEMS $1.00
Kenneth Patchen, POEMS OF HUMOR AND PROTEST $1.00
Pablo Picasso, HUNK OF SKIN $1.00
Tom Pickard, GUTTERSNIPE $2.50
Charles Plymell, LAST OF THE MOCCASINS $3.00
Janine Pommy-Vega, POEMS TO FERNANDO $1.25
Jacques Prévert, PAROLES $1.00
Kenneth Rexroth, THIRTY SPANISH POEMS OF LOVE & EXILE $1.00
Charles & Janet Richards, CLASSIC CHINESE & JAPANESE COOKING $1.50

Ed Sanders, POEM FROM JAIL 75¢
Paul Jordan Smith, A KEY TO THE ULYSSES OF JAMES JOYCE $1.50
Carl Solomon, MISHAPS, PERHAPS $1.50
Carl Solomon, MORE MISHAPS $1.50
Italo Svevo, JAMES JOYCE $1.25
Roland Topor, PANIC $1.00
Charles Upton, PANIC GRASS $1.00
Andre Voznesensky, DOGALYPSE $1.50
Arthur Waley, THE NINE SONGS $2.50
Alan W. Watts, BEAT ZEN, SQUARE ZEN, AND ZEN $1.00
Walt Whitman, AN AMERICAN PRIMER $1.50
William Carlos Williams, KORA IN HELL: IMPROVISATIONS $1.50
Colin Wilson, POETRY & MYSTICISM $2.00
Pete Winslow, A DAISY IN THE MEMORY OF A SHARK $2.00
Yevtushenko, Voznesensky & Kirsanov, RED CATS $1.00

BY ALLEN GINSBERG

Poetry Books

Howl and Other Poems. City Lights Books, 1956. favorite
Kaddish and Other Poems. City Lights Books, 1961.
Empty Mirror; Early Poems. Totem-Corinth Books, 1961.
Reality Sandwiches. City Lights Books, 1963.
Ankor Wat. Fulcrum Press, 1968.
Airplane Dreams. Anansi/City Lights Books, 1968.
Planet News. City Lights Books, 1968.
Gates of Wrath; Rhymed Poems 1948-1952. Grey Fox Press, 1972.
The Fall of America; Poems of these States 1965-1971. City Lights, 1973.
Iron Horse. Coach House Press/City Lights, 1974.

Prose Books

Yage Letters. (with Wm. S. Burroughs), City Lights Books, 1963.
Indian Journals. Dave Haselwood/City Lights Books, 1970.
Improvised Poetics. Anonym Books, 1971.
Gay Sunshine Interview. Grey Fox Press, 1974.

Phonograph Records

Howl and Other Poems. Fantasy-Galaxy Records, No. 7013.
Wm. Blake's Songs of Innocence and of Experience Tuned by Allen Ginsberg. MGM/Verve Records. FTS - 3083, 1970.